Family History Case Studies

Edmund (Ned) Collins
1817 - 1862
The Convict Baker's Boy

Christine Sutton Dip. Family History

A Business and Property Training Queensland Publication

Foreword

"You are our living link to the past. Tell your grandchildren the story of the struggles waged, at home and abroad. Of sacrifices made for freedom's sake. And tell them your own story as well — because [everybody] has a story to tell."

George H.W. Bush

Genealogy is defined by the Oxford dictionary as *"A line of descent traced continuously from an ancestor."* Traditionally, genealogists use vital records and sound documentary evidence to trace back from a single individual to their earliest recorded ancestor, in a direct line on a Family Tree. The emphasis is often on how many generations there are on the tree; how high it has grown, how many branches there are and how wide it is spread. The tree is the focus.

Family Historians, on the other hand, focus on people, on who their ancestors were, when and where they lived, how they lived, what they did, and why they made their life choices. They look for what has made their descendants the people they are today. Family Historians It is the driving force behind the television series, "Who do you think you are?" The emphasis is on the fruit rather than the tree.

Neither of these approaches can stand alone. Family Historians need to practice good genealogical research. They need to follow the basic principles of genealogy in order to find the ancestor and tell their story. Family History brings another dimension to genealogy. It enriches it.

Edmund (Ned) Collins, the Baker's Boy of Berkshire, is a case study in tracing convict ancestors. The mystery surrounding Ned has taken 35 years to solve. The search began in 1984, long before there were digitised records. Finding Ned took hours of research in the New South Wales Archives Office, the Mitchell Library and the NSW Registry Office. With the birth of technology and the Internet, research became easier, but no less time consuming, and far more expensive. The role of Ancestry.com, New South Wales State Records, University of Tasmania and LINC Tasmania have been invaluable in bringing down the brick wall that surrounded Ned Collins, but Ancestry.com and like services come at a price, and any BMD certificates are an additional cost to the service.When needing to use online services that involve expensive subscriptions, it is vital that Family Historians make every search count, and know where the free searches are available. Throughout Ned's story you will find chunks of information on process, tips and hints on how and where I found clues to the mystery, where the free sources of Convict records can be found and how persistence and patience can remove bricks from the genealogical wall.

It is my hope that not you will not only find this book helpful in overcoming your inevitable brick walls and finding new sources of information, but that you will discover a little more about the life and times of ordinary people in a very vibrant period of Australian history.

Granny Smith

M. Christine Sutton

In the beginning...

We start our journey, as all good family historians do, at the beginning, with what was known in 1984; the Line of Ancestry and Tree of Descendancy from the present generation to the Baker's Boy of Berkshire.

Garçon Boulanger

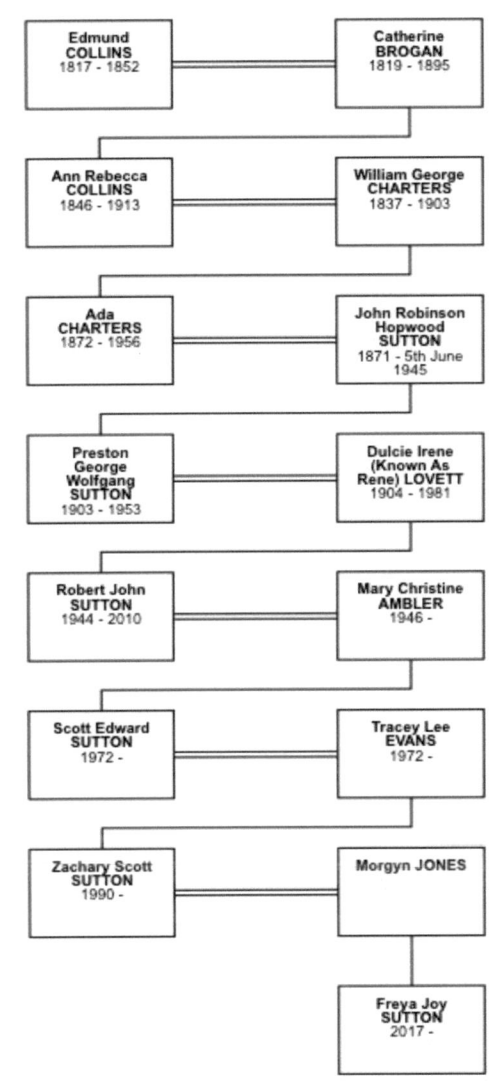

**Line of Ancestry from
Freya Joy SUTTON to Edmund COLLINS**

Freya Joy SUTTON b: 09 Sep 2017

- Zachary Scott SUTTON b: 10 Dec 1990 in Bulli, New South Wales, Australia
- Scott Edward SUTTON b: 18 Jun 1972 in Wollongong, New South Wales, Australia
- Robert John SUTTON b: 18 Jun 1944 in Campsie, NSW, Australia, d: 14 Jun 2010 in Newcastle, New South Wales, Australia
- Preston George Wolfgang SUTTON b: 11 Jul 1903 in Redfern, NSW, Australia, d: 27 Jun 1953 in Thirroul, NSW, Australia; Age: 49
- Ada CHARTERS b: 06 Nov 1872 in Tambaroora, New South Wales; Also known as Lal, d: 19 Oct 1956 in Sydney, New South Wales, Australia
- Ann Rebecca COLLINS b: 20 May 1846 in Campbelltown, New South Wales, d: 28 Jul 1913 in Wallerawang, New South Wales, Australia
- Edmund COLLINS b: 1817 in West Horsley, Surrey, England, d: 1852 in Sofala, New South Wa

The first principle of genealogical research is "Start with what you already know".

Before I started on my research, I had all of the vital records for Robert, his parents and his grandparents. The next step was to use the information on the death record of his grandmother, Ada Charters, to search for the records of her parents. From those records, I could be sure that each time I identified an ancestor I was as sure as it was possible to be that this was the correct person.

It is very easy, using such services as Ancestry.com and Family Search, to take other people's research as recorded on their Family Tree as correct. This is unwise. Unless that person has obtained and can provide the vital records of the ancestor it may, or may not, be correct. I have found, many times over, that an existing tree shows a completely different Ann Collins to Robert's Great Grandmother. This creates a link to our family that doesn't exist. If I had followed those trees blindly, I would never have found Ned Collins, for the other Ann came to Australia as a Bounty Immigrant and was not born in Campbelltown.

The search begins

Ned Collins first appeared on the family tree in 1983. I had been researching Robert Sutton's paternal ancestry and found that his grandmother, Ada Charters, had been born in 1872 at Sofala, NSW,[1] just after the gold rush. In 1983 there was no Internet, no online searches. Research involved visiting the local Registry Office, manually filling in the forms and paying for a search of the records. Then waiting for a result, if any, for weeks. NSW Registry Office came back with her birth certificate identifying her parents as Ann Collins and William Charters. Next step, go back to the registry office and request a search for birth certificates for each of them. Ann's certificate came back. She was born in 1846 in Campbelltown, NSW, and her parents were Edmund Collins and Catherine Brogan. No birth record could be found of William Charters.

Continuing the search, I requested a search for certificates for Edmund and Catherine, but there were no birth records. My assumption, then, was that William, Edmund and Catherine must have been immigrants. I would need to search the immigration and shipping records. This meant catching the train to Sydney to visit the NSW Archives; sitting for hours scrolling through microfilm and microfiche. It was a long hard slog. After several days travelling to Sydney from Wollongong and sitting all day in the archives trolling through the card indices and the microfilms I found Catherine. There was no sign of Edmund. However, I did manage to find their marriage in St Francis' Parish records in Wollongong.[2] Edmund's name was shortened to Ned.

What did I already know? I knew Ned was in Wollongong in 1843 when he married Catherine. I knew they had a child in Campbelltown in 1846. At this point I turned to the history of Campbelltown and found a reference to Ned Collins, a baker, in Campbelltown. It could be him. However, try as I might, I could not find any further trace of Edmund or Ned Collins prior to 1843. I came up against my genealogical brick wall.

By this time it was about 1986. Email was not yet an option - Australia had no email services. The Internet was not yet invented, searching was still a manual task, but electronic record storage, if you built your own database (which I taught myself to do), was possible. Our family tree grew exponentially, and yet still there was no sign of Edmund "Ned" Collins in any of the shipping records or birth records. I set Ned aside for some years to pursue another, rather fascinating ancestor. Over that period, online searching was born. Yet, still no sign of Ned could be found.It was to be almost twenty five years later that the "Convict Permissions To Marry" index was released on Ancestry.com. Even though I had been unable to find Ned Collins in convict records, I took a punt and searched this index using the term 'Edmund Collins AND Catherine Brogan'. Nothing. I tried 'Catherine Brogan'. Nothing. I tried 'Edmund Collins', BINGO! There he was, Edmund Collins requesting permission to marry Catherine ROGAN.[3] A simple misspelling could have put another brick in the wall. Instead, the wall came tumbling down to reveal the story of the Sutton family's First Arrival, and their heritage as descendants of a British convict.

I have traced Ned back through the gold fields, Goulburn, Campbelltown, Sydney, convict ships, prison hulks and courtrooms to Berkshire. This is his story, through time, place and history, as best we can piece it together.

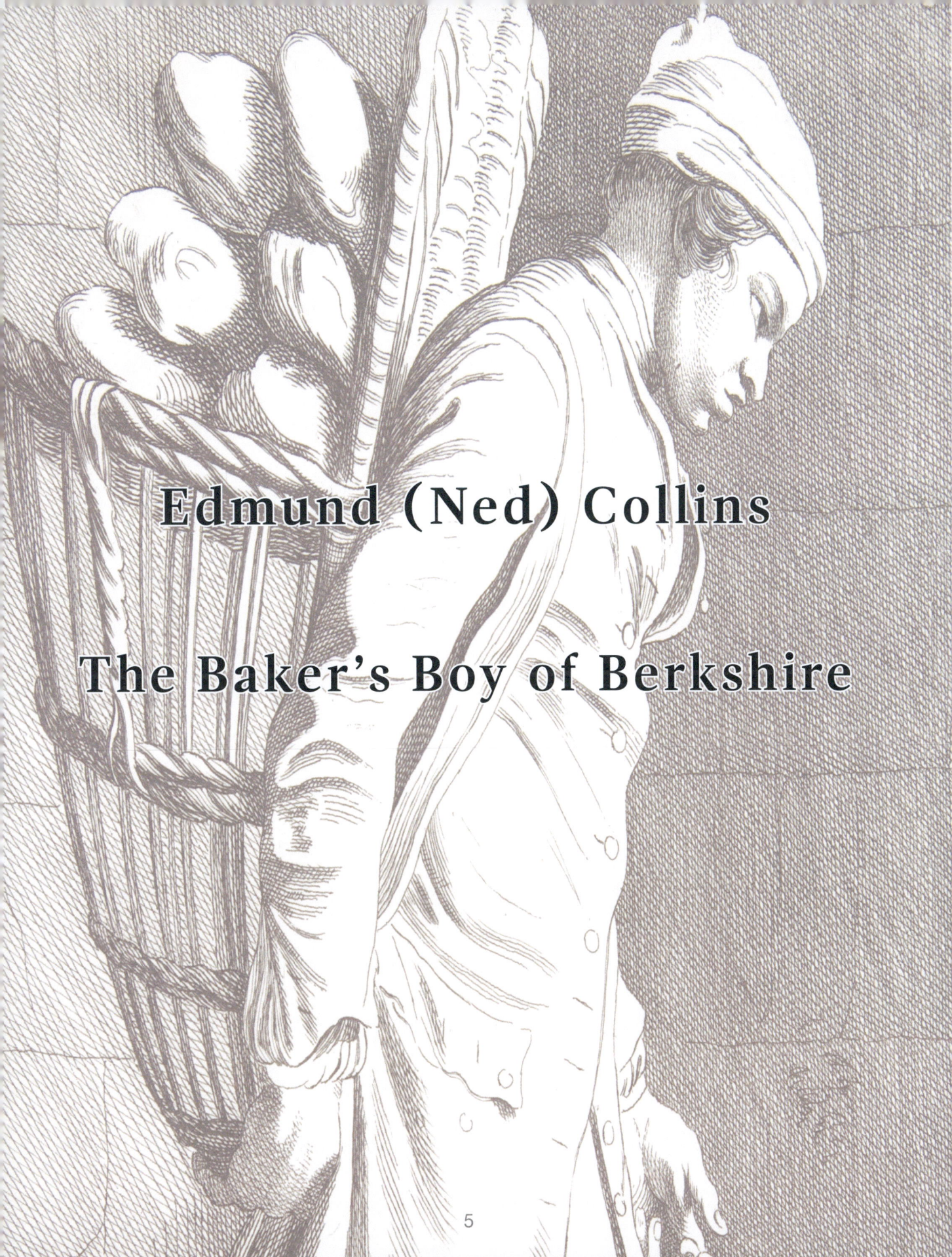

Edmund (Ned) Collins

The Baker's Boy of Berkshire

In 1835, Edmund Collins, known to his friends as Ned, was 18 years old. We have no idea of exactly where Ned lived, or what his life was like prior to that year. The first mention of him that we can find is in the court records and newspapers of March 1835. [4]

From these we know that he was a "baker's boy", an apprentice baker, and came from Berkshire. We have not found any record of him in that county; however, in 1832, there was a baker by the name of Edmund Collins in Short Street, New Windsor. He was too old to be our Edmond. We have a copy of his will from 1852, by which time Ned was in NSW. There is no evidence of a link, but families often employed relatives in the family trade, so it could be that this was Edmond's father or uncle. The lack of a documentary evidence of an Edmond Collins born between 1816 and 1818 in Berkshire means we cannot be sure of any relationship with this baker of the same name. However, there is primary source evidence of an Edmond Collins, born in the right year, in Surrey, which is the next county to Berkshire.[5] He is the son of Edmund Collins, a miller, of West Horsley, so he was living within the bread making industry. We have the church record of he and his two brothers being baptised on the same day in 1819,[6] when Edmund was a year and a half old. It is more than likely that this *is* our Ned, but, all that we can be sure of is that Ned Collins worked as a baker's boy in Berkshire in the period leading up to March 1835.

What work did a baker's boy do? What would his day be like? To find out required research into 19th Century apprenticeships and bakeries. [7]

To find the answers to these questions, we need to go back to a time when there was no electricity or gas to heat ovens, no machinery to mix and make the dough, no slicing machines to cut it up and no plastic wrappers to keep it clean on the shelves.

There were no large factory bakeries in 1835, nor were there any large shops or supermarkets selling a variety of products. Milk came from the dairy; shoes came from the cobbler; clothes came from the dressmaker or tailor; fruit and vegetables from the market. Bread was made and sold in a bakery.

The village bakery was a small shop. About the same size as a 'Baker's Delight or 'Brumby's Bakery' shop. The oven was small compared to those used today. As for the fuel, it was the same as the Romans used: dried bundles of sticks kindled with a tinderbox. The fire was lit inside the oven, then raked out once the oven was hot. As there was no thermostat, it needed an experienced eye to know when it was ready to bake. The baker probably worked alone with a 'boy' to help him. Bakers in larger towns often employed 'journeyman bakers' - bakers who knew how to make bread and puddings but did not own a shop. They were paid a small wage. The apprentice baker, the baker's boy, was the lowest paid and hardest worked in the bakery.

How did bakers in the 19th century make bread?

There isn't a lot needed to make bread; flour, yeast, hands and little knowledge. Making a batch of bread could take between 3 and ten hours. It had to be mixed, left to rise, kneaded and left to rise again and then baked. In the early part of the 1900s, most bread was brown. Flour was not as refined and bleached as today's. The bread was not as light and soft as ours.

The flour was stone ground by the village miller and came in 20-stone (126 kg) sacks. That's seven times heavier than modern health and safety rules allow, but Ned and his employer humped them single-handedly.

The yeast came from beer. Today's commercial bakers rely on dried yeast, but the baker Ned worked for would have bought buckets of frothy brewer's yeast from the local brewery. Called 'ale-barm', this made a sweet-tasting bread. Ned would have carried the buckets from the brewery to the bakery, and they were very heavy.

It took a skillful baker to judge the right amount of ale-barm to mix with the flour and make a golden, crusty loaf of bread. It was unpredictable, and the bread could go wonky. It might turn out sloppy, and the loaves come out lopsided. Once the bread was made, it had to be sold door to door. This was one of Ned's jobs. He would set out with a basket of bread on his back each day to visit the regular customers and look for new ones.

The average price of a 2lb loaf was fourpence and one farthing; a quarter of an agricultural worker's daily wages. It was a lot for poor people to pay. Ned needed to be nice to customers and give them value for their money. If the bread was not golden and crusty and fresh, the baker's customers would either find another baker to buy from or make their own bread at home.

Bakery work hours were long, starting in the early hours of the morning or very late at night. Ned had a tiring job, requiring strength and stamina. But in 1835, Ned's life changed, and not for the better.

In 1835 Ned appeared in the Crown Court at the Northampton Assizes charged with Highway Robbery. He was about to learn how hard life could be.

The County Goal, between the Sessions house and the Infirmary. It has a garden behind it and a pleasant view of the Country.

What would bring an apprentice baker before the courts?

What would make him turn to crime?

Why was the Workhouse such a dreaded fate? By the early 1830s the established system of poor relief was proving to be unsustainable. The New Poor Law of 1834 discouraged the provision of relief to anyone who refused to enter a workhouse.

Life in a workhouse was intended to be harsh, to deter the able-bodied poor and to ensure that only the truly destitute would apply. In *The State of the Poor*, [11] Frederick Eden wrote;

"The workhouse is an inconvenient building, with small windows, low rooms and dark staircases. It is surrounded by a high wall, that gives it the appearance of a prison, and prevents free circulation of air. There are 8 or 10 beds in each room, chiefly of flocks, and consequently retentive of all scents and very productive of vermin. The passages are in great want of whitewashing. No regular account is kept of births and deaths, but when smallpox, measles or malignant fevers make their appearance in the house, the mortality is very great."

This was the time of the Industrial and Agricultural Revolutions. Farmers were being forced off their land, and agricultural workers were abandoning their jobs in the countryside. They were moving into the towns to find work in the new factories. As a result, towns were growing, and so was poverty. Bread is an essential part of life. The poorest people sometimes made rusks out of the baker's floor sweepings, boiling them into a pudding. Times were tough. Bakers were relied upon to feed the population, but there was a problem.

By this time, all but the destitute were asking for white bread. Grinding white flour takes longer, and costs more than brown. The baker had to pay more for his flour, but competition was so fierce the baker could not charge more for a loaf. Putting 'fillers' into the bread to replace some of the expensive flour was common. Alum, a chemical compound, was added to bread to whiten it, meaning the baker could use some brown flour. This was bad for people. Alum slows down the absorption of nutrients and causes diarrhoea. Children sometimes died. Potatoes, plaster of Paris and sawdust were also used to bulk up loaves. At the same time, a growing middle class was demanding fresh bread for breakfast, so bakers now had to work all night. It was back-breaking, and their lives were often short. Bakers needed every customer they could get, and competition is vicious. Their business costs were high, and the customers were few. They were finding it hard to make a living. It is was even more difficult for the baker's boy. [8]

The 1830s were not a good time to be a baker's apprentice. The apprenticeship scheme had broken down, and many apprentices in many trades were underpaid, overworked and often subject to abuse by their employers.

This newspaper clipping is from a British newspaper published around the time Ned was working as a bakers boy.[9] It illustrates the abuse that could be meted it out to these unfortunate souls.

There were reports of an increase in violence in the rural areas of England. The Poor Laws had been reviewed and Workhouses were created as the solution to dealing with the overwhelming numbers of poor and unemployed. Conditions in the Workhouses were so bad that many of the poor found other ways to survive than falling on the dubious mercy of the Workhouse Governors.

At Sunbury Petty Sessions William Thomas Nash, 25, a baker, of Laleham-road, Staines, was charged with assaulting and beating Egbert Allen, fifteen years of age, by striking him on the body with a whip-stock. Prisoner pleaded "Guilty," and elected to be dealt with summarily. John Warricker, a builder's foreman, said the prisoner struck the boy a number of times with the whip, and then he struck him full in the face with his fist and knocked him down. Afterwards witness found that the boy was bruised from head to foot, and his right eye was bleeding profusely. Witness therefore took the boy to the police station where he was examined by a doctor, and later prisoner was charged. Police-constable Scott said he arrested prisoner, and in answer to witness he said: " Yes; I gave him a —— good thrashing with the handle of a whip. He has been neglecting my customers." After a short consultation, the Bench sentenced the prisoner to two months' hard labour, without the option of a fine. Mr. Young said, under the circumstances, prisoner was entitled to appeal against the decision of the Court, and there were persons in court who would enter into recognizances for the appearance of his client at the next quarter sessions. The Bench allowed the appeal, and the Rev. G. V. Briscoe and Mr. Charles Tolley, a master baker, of Staines, were accepted as sureties.

Whether these conditions, and his own circumstances caused Edmund to turn to crime to survive, we will never know. However, turn to crime he did, and by 7th March 1835, he was in goal and on trial for Highway Robbery.

Robbery, or attempted robbery of any kind, was defined as;

> *"An open and violent assault, resulting in the forcible removal of property of any value from the victim, and putting him or her in fear."* [10]

The punishment was usually imprisonment, flogging or transportation

Highway robbery was a capital offence for which the penalty would be either Life Imprisonment or Death. It was distinguished from "Robbery" as being;

> *"...a robbery which took place on or near the King's Highway"*

We tend to think of Highway Robbery as a crime committed by a dashing figure, mounted on a rearing horse crying,
> *"Stand and deliver! Your money or your life!"*

Many of us have childhood memories of the poem "The Highwayman", and can possibly quote such lines as;
> *"The highway came riding, riding, riding,*
> *The Highwayman came riding,*
> *Up to the old inn door."*

In 1835 this was far from the reality. Improvements in policing, transport, banking and credit had all but done away with mounted highway robbery. Only isolated incidents of robbery by gangs of footpads occurred in the early 19th century.

Indeed, in the eight years from 1830 to 1838 only three highway robbery cases were tried at the Old Bailey. The last recorded robbery by a mounted highwayman occurred in 1831.

 However, the Industrial Revolution had created great poverty and an increase in crime. Law makers believed that the deterrent to violent crime should remain and, when Ned stood trial in 1835, the compulsory penalty for robbery with violence and highway robbery was death by hanging.

> *Edmund Collins*, aged 18, *James Turner*, 36, & *William Brown*, 20, charged with having, on the King's highway in the parish of Dodford, feloniously assaulted *Joseph York*, and stolen from his person three sovereigns and 15s. in silver.

> Judgment of Death was recorded against *Edmund Collins*, aged 18, *James Turner*, aged 36, and *Wm. Brown*, aged 20, for having robbed Joseph York of £3. 15s. on the highway, at Dodford.
> *Thomas Dodson*, aged 46, was acquitted on a charge of stealing a half-crown, belonging to Samuel Bull, of Cottingham.
> *George Taylor*, aged 22, a sheep-stealer, was sentenced to seven years' transportation.

Northampton Mercury March 1835

On the 7th March, 1835, Edmund Collins and his co-accused, William Brown, aged 20 and James Taylor, aged 35, were brought before the court at the Northampton Spring Quarter Sessions.

The trial took place in the Northampton Assizes house, which still stands today.   The courtroom is still as it was in 1835.

19th Century trials were quite different from trials today. The accused person was expected to provide proof of innocence. They did not always have a lawyer to represent them. It must have been a terrifying experience for a boy of 18 to appear before the magistrate and hear the sentence of death passed on him and his two friends.

They would have been tried together. Their trial would have started with the clerk reading the charge. In the case of Ned and his companions this was;

> *"...having on the King's highway in the parish of Dodford, feloniously assaulted Joseph York, and stolen from his person three sovereigns and 15s. in silver."*[13]

The prosecutor would then have presented the case against the defendant, followed by the witnesses, who testified under oath. Witness testimony was the most common source of evidence and judges frequently intervened to ask questions or comment. The defendant was then asked to state his or her case. They could call witnesses, if they had any, and use a defence lawyer.

After the judge's summing up, the jury would have retired to consider the verdicts. In some courts, cases were tried in batches, with juries hearing perhaps half a dozen trials before retiring to consider their verdicts. Each day a new jury was sworn in.

At the end of the session, those prisoners who had been found guilty were brought forward to hear their punishments. Defendants who were convicted of capital crimes were given a chance to address the Court before they were sentenced.

The judge would then pass sentence. In the case of issuing the death penalty, the judge would say:

"The court doth order you to be taken from hence to the place from whence you came, and thence to the place of execution, and that you be hanged by the neck until you are dead, and that your body be afterward buried within the precincts of the prison in which you shall be confined after your conviction. And may the Lord have mercy upon your soul."

At the start of the 19th century, the sentence of death on a prisoner was often recorded after the guilty verdict, but the sentence carried out was transportation or imprisonment. This happened because many of the magistrates felt that the compulsory death sentence was too harsh. For about 60% of offences punishable by the death sentence, the magistrates recorded capital punishment, then gave a less serious one. As the century went on, the number of people who were sentenced to be hanged decreased.

Ned and his companions had their death sentence recorded and then commuted to transportation. Ned Collins, James Turner and William Brown were to be transported to the colonies, to serve a term of 14 years in New South Wales. It was quite a severe penalty. While not trivial, their crime was not as heinous as those of many criminals receiving lesser periods of transportation. At this time, the period of transportation for most convicts was seven to ten years.

However, I doubt that Ned would have argued with it, 14 years in a penal colony was better than hanging by the neck until he was dead.

> The following convicts were removed from our county gaol, yesterday se'nnight, in order to be put on board the Leviathan Hulk, at Portsmouth. John Haynes, Joseph Russell, Thomas Steanes, and Samuel Dawes, under sentence of transportation for life; James Short, George Cox, William Moyses, Joseph Calcutt, Norman Smith, the younger, Edmund Collins, James Turner, William Brown, for fourteen years; John Lane and Geo. Taylor, for seven years.

Just over a week after his trial this notice appeared in the Northampton Mercury, *(yesterday se'night meaning a week ago from yesterday).*

Edmund Collins, James Turner and William Brown were taken to the Portsmouth to await transportation. Ned's long journey to Australia had begun.

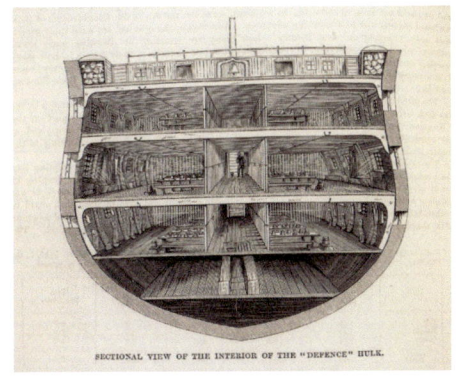

SECTIONAL VIEW OF THE INTERIOR OF THE "DEFENCE" HULK.

No.	Name	Age	Crime	Where & When Convd	Sentence	How disposed of
	From Ilchester 11 May 1835					
1572	Henry Hornblower	19		Wells 23 March 1835	7	N.S.W. 22 Oct 18..
1573	Pat Jno Jennings	23	H.d Watch	Do 23 "	7	" 22 "
1574	Isaac Wilcox	41	Rec.g Ho..	Do 23 "	7	" 22 "
1575	Willm Griffiths	28		Taunton 31 "	Life	" 1 June
1576	Robt Norvil	57	Cattle Std	Do 31 "	Life	" 22 July
1577	Willm Braddick	20	Sheepstg	Do 31 "	Life	" 22 "
1578	David Rose	57	Housebd	Do 31 "	Life	" 22 "
1579	William Poole	17		Do 31 "	14	N.S.W 31 Aug
1580	James Trevor	17	Housebd	Do 31 "	Life	N.S.W 22 July
1581	Joseph Bellamy	19	Do	Do 31 "	Life	" 22 "
1582	Wm Ludlow	27	Burglary	Do 31 "	Life	" 22 "
1583	John Blueford	19	Housebd	Do 31 "	Life	" 22 "
	From Bodmin 12 May 1835					
1584	Fredk Smith	18	Housebd	Launceston 24 March 1835	14	" 19 Oct
1585	Geo Withington	22	Coining	Do 24 "	Life	" 19 "
1586	Joseph Nelson	26	Do	Do 24 "	7	" 19 "
1587	James Hall	30	H.d Watch	Do 24 "	7	" 19 "
1588	John Richards	23		Do 24 "	7	" 22 July
1589	William Davis	18	Housebd	Do 24 "	14	" 1 June
	From Cambridge 13 May 1835					
1590	William Skinner	18	H.o Robbd	Cambridge 18 March 1835	Life	" 1 "
1591	John Barton	32	Do	Do 18 "	Life	" 19 Oct
1592	Henry Barton	24	Do	Do 18 "	Life	" 19 "
1593	Thomas Reynolds	23	Do	Do 18 "	Life	" 19 "
	From York 14 May 1835					
1594	Jno Middleton	30	Felony	Sheffield 26 March 1835	7	" 19 "
1595	Patrick Peace	15	H.breakg	Do 26 "	7	" 1 June
1596	George Slater	28	H.d W.d App	Pontefract 9 April "	7	" 19 Oct
1597	Will Proctor	32	Sheepstg	York 28 March "	Life	Died 25 May
1598	Emanuel Haley	41	Housestg	Do 28 "	Life	N.S.W. 19 Oct
1599	George Walker	27	Do	Do 28 "	Life	" 6 Feb
1600	Chas Spencer alias ...			Beverly 13 April "	7	" 19 Oct 18..
1601	William Whittle	24		Pontefract 13 "	7	" 19 "
1602	George Milner	23	Stealing	Do 13 "	7	" 19 "
1603	John Waites	21	Housestg	Beverly 13 "	Life	" 6 Feb
1604	George Budd	19	Housebkg	Leeds 20 "	7	" 19 Oct
1605	Samuel Barnett	22	Do	Do 20 "	14	" 6 Feb
1606	Thos Elliston	16	H.d Trespass	Do 20 "	7	" 1 June
	From H.M.S. Victory 14 May 1835					
1607	Martin Gorman	22		Jamaica 8 Decr 1834	14	V.D. 15 June
1608	John Malley	24	Do	Do 8 "	Life	" 15 "
1609	John Brown	23	Do	Do 8 "	Life	" 15 "
1610	Patrick Mangan	26		Do Do "	14	N.S.W 22 July
	From Biddeford 21 May 1835					
1611	William Arthur	15	Stealing	Biddeford 4 May 1835	7	" 1 June
	From Newgate 27 May 1835					
1612	Charles Treneman	19	H.o fm Perso	Newgate 6 April 1835	7	V.D. 31 Aug 1835
1613	Timothy Grady	18	Do	Do 6 "	7	N.S.W 1 June
1614	James Neal	19	Do	Do 6 "	7	V.D. 31 Aug
1615	John Larkin	18	Do	Do 6 "	7	N.S.W 1 June
1616	Elijah Lazarus	29	St.g Silk Gds	Do 6 "	Life	N.S.W 19 Oct
1617	James Brannam	22	Steal.g Dry Goods	Do 6 "	7	" 6 Feb 1836
1618	Geo Chas Griffiths	19	St.g Money	Do 6 "	14	" 6 "
1619	Thos Bellamy	19	St.g fm Perso	Do 6 "	7	" 22 July 18..
1620	George Martin	18	St.g Kings	Do 6 "	7	" 1 June
1621	Thomas Williams	24	St.g fm Perso	Do 6 "	Life	" 1 "
1622	Thomas Pitman	21	H.o Stolen Gds	Do 6 "	7	" 19 Oct
1623	William Taylor	46	St.g Hay	Do 6 "	7	" 19 "
1624	Jas Thos Richards	20	St.g W..	Do 6 "	7	" 22 July
1625	James Moody	37	H.g fm.n Boots	Do 6 "	7	" 19 Oct
1626	Abraham Abrahams	45	Fraud	Do 6 "	7	" 19 "
1627	John Hedge	25	Uttering	Do 6 "	7	" 1 June
1628	Thos Woodcock	25	St.g fm Perso	Do 6 "	7	" 19 Oct
1629	George Fisher	30	Receiving	Do 6 "	14	" 6 Feb 1835
1630	Will Brown	20	Felony	Do 6 "	14	" 19 Oct 1835
1631	John Brien	27	St.g S.oo C	Do 6 "	7	" 1 June
1632	Thomas Gion	20	St.g a Necklace	Do 6 "	7	" 6 Feb 1835
1633	Willm Thomas	24	H.a Follr.n	Westminster 2 "	7	" 6 Feb 1835
1634	John Davis	31	St.g fm h Lance	Do 2 "	7	N.S.W 19 Oct 1835
1635	Daniel Sullivan	23	St.g fm Perso	Do 2 "	7	" 6 Feb 1836
1636	Samuel Tilk	36	H.g 4 Hats	Newgate 11 May "	14	V.D. 31 Aug 1835
	From Horsham 1 June 1835					
1637	Jno Smith	16	St.g Coals	Lewes 20 May 1835	Life	N.S.W 22 July
1638	John North	24	H.d Watch	Do 20 "	Life	" 6 Feb 1836
1639	Will Holliday	42	St.g a Bridle	Do 20 "	Life	V.D. 31 Aug 1835
1640	Will Pollard	21	St.g Bridle	Do 20 "	Life	N.S.W 19 Oct
1641	John Elliott	19	H.g 22 Bushells	Do 20 "	14	" 19 "
1642	George Camp	28	by false pretences	Do 20 "	7	Remit 13 July
	From Northampton 6 June 1835					
1643	James Street	20	St.g a Watch	Northampton 2 Mar 1835	14	N.S.W 6 Feb 1836
1644	George Cox	42	St.g Ducks	Do 2 "	14	
1645	William Menzies	35	St.g Tools	Do 2 "	14	N.S.W 6 Feb 1836
1646	George Taylor	20	Killing a Sheep	Do 2 "	7	" 6 "
1647	Joseph Calcutt	21	Housebd	Do 8 Jan 1835	14	" 6 "
1648	John Lane	60	St.g Wood	Do 8 "	7	" 6 "
1649	Samuel Dawes	26	H.d a Bag	Do 9 April	Life	" 6 "
1650	Thos Stearnes	23	Hogstg	Do 9 "	Life	" 29 Oct
1651	John Haynes	24	Sheepstg	Do 9 "	Life	" 19 Oct 1835
1652	Joseph Walsall	21	Steal.g a ..	Do 9 "	Life	" 19 "
1653	Norman Smith	13	Wooden Bottle	Do 9 "	14	" 22 July
1654	Edmund Collins	18	H. Robbd	Do 2 March	14	" 19 Oct
1655	James Turner	36	Do	Do 2 "	14	" 6 Feb 1836
1656	William Brown	19	Do	Do 2 "	14	" 19 Oct 1835

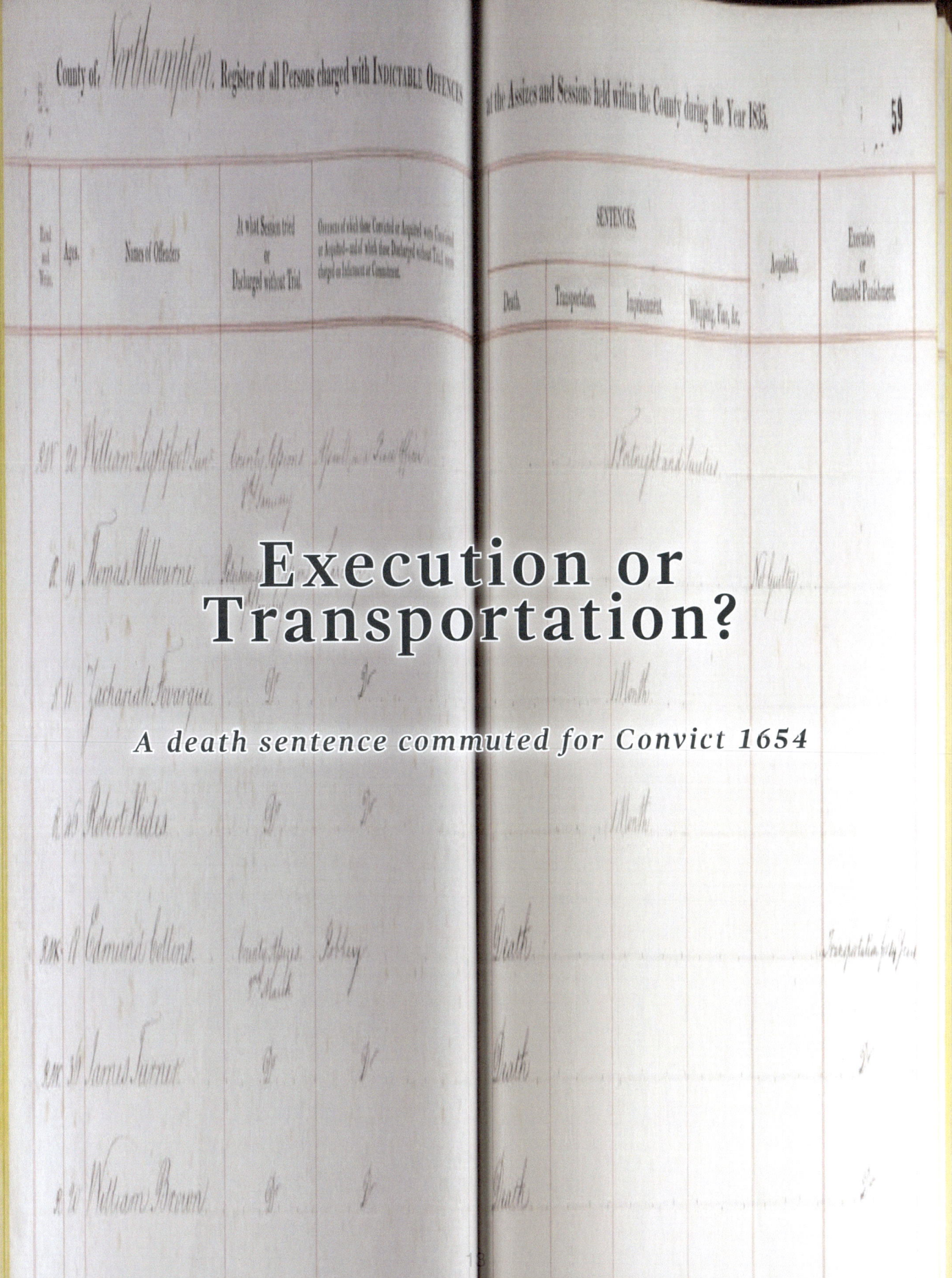

Execution or Transportation?

A death sentence commuted for Convict 1654

Prison hulks were old navy ships, anchored along the banks of the Thames and in some ports such as Portsmouth and Plymouth. English prisons were becoming so crowded, that it was decided to use them as gaols. The In 1776, the English Parliament authorised their use for a two year period. They continued to house prisoners for the next 82 years!

A list of the prisoners was kept for each hulk; their name, age, crime, place of trial, sentence and disposal (where they went to on leaving the hulk). These records for some of the prison hulks of the early 1800s can be found in the British Archives. They are a mine of information for those researching Convict Ancestors.

Ned was transferred first from Northampton Goal to Newgate Prison.

On 27th March, 1835, he was taken aboard the prison hulk, *Leviathan,* moored in Plymouth Harbour. He was given a number - prisoner number 1654. There he would await his transportation to NSW.

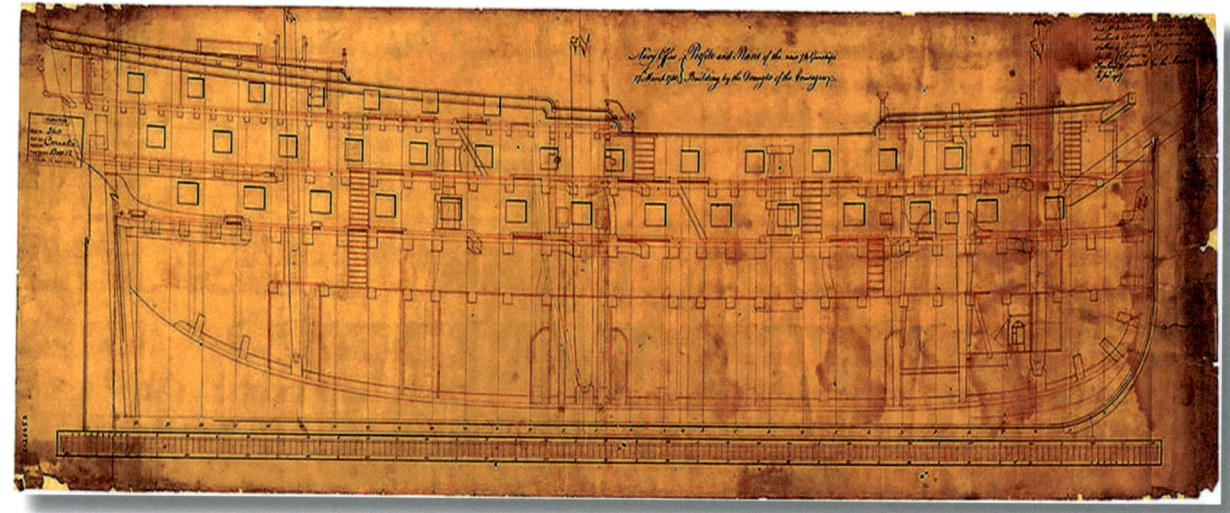

HMS Leviathan - original plans 1790

Loading prisoners to a hulk at Plymouth

On most hulks, living conditions and the treatment of convicts were appalling and far worse than in the prisons. In the daytime, the convicts were put to hard labour. At night they were chained to their bunks to prevent them from escaping.

Convicts could be punished for crimes on board by being placed in heavy irons or flogged. The standards of hygiene were so poor that outbreaks of disease spread quickly. Typhoid and cholera were common, and there was a high death rate amongst the prisoners.

However, Ned was in luck. Leviathan had a health and hygiene routine that was used as an example to other prisons and hulks across the country. The better-than-average conditions on the Leviathan can be attributed to the supervision of naval surgeon superintendants, who were introduced into the hulks in the early years of the 19th Century.

These surgeons were highly skilled in keeping men healthy at sea. They had developed hygiene, dietary and health practices that were designed to combat disease and avoid such dietary related issues as scurvy. What's more, as naval officers they had authority and respect aboard His Majesty's ships and, in matters of convict health and shipboard hygeine, outranked the captain of the vessel.

In 1838 a report on the condition of the Leviathan and the prisoners aboard was made by Mr J. H. Capper, Superintendent of Ships and Vessels Employed for the Confinement of Offenders Under Sentence of Transportation. [14] It is likely that the conditions and treatment received by Edmund were very similar to those described in the report.

Ned's daily life would have been very much as follows.

" The behaviour of the convicts is generally represented as extremely orderly, both as to the observance of their employment and of their moral and religious duties. Following is an extract showing the mode of treating them, and the manner of life to which these unfortunates are necessarily subjected. Thus the following is a return of the daily proceedings on board the Leviathan convict hulk, at Portsmouth, August 16, 1838, being the example :

At three o'clock all the cooks are let up to boil the prisoners' breakfast ; at half past five all hands are called up; at a quarter before six the prisoners are mustered, after which breakfast is served down, then one of the three decks is washed, which is done every morning alternately. At a quarter before seven the prisoners (each one bringing his hammock and stowing it away on deck) proceed to labour. On leaving the hulk their irons are examined by the guards, who also search their persons, to prevent any thing improper being concealed; and in order that they may be more strict in the execution of this duty, in the event of anything being afterwards found upon a prisoner, the guard that searched him is made responsible.

The prisoners are divided into ten divisions, each of which is subdivided and delivered into the charge of dock-yard labourers. The prisoners are overlooked by the first and second mate, who patrol the yard, not only to prevent them from straying from their division or attempting to escape, but to make all parties attend strictly to their duties.

At a quarter of an hour previous to the return of the prisoners on shore from labour, those employed on board are mustered, to ascertain whether the number is right. At twelve the prisoners return from labour, are searched to prevent any part of the public stores being brought out of the dock-yard, after which a general muster takes place, the dinners are served down, and the prisoners are locked up in their respective wards. A watch, consisting of an officer and half of the ship's company, is set on between decks, where they remain till forty minutes past twelve, when the other half relieves them. At twenty minutes past one the prisoners resume their labour, and at a quarter before six return on board; their irons are examined and their persons searched as in the forenoon. At halfpast six o'clock school commences, and at half-past seven prayers are read in the chapel; after which they are mustered and locked up in their respective wards for the night.

The ship's company are divided into three watches (one of which is absent every night, unless duty requires it on board, and returns on board next morning half an hour before the prisoners proceed to labour. New prisoners are made to pass along the quarter deck every morning with their hats off, for a fortnight after their arrival, in the presence of the officers and guards, that their features, gait, &c. may be made familiar to them, in case of any attempting disguise to effect an escape.

On Saturday evening every prisoner washes his person thoroughly before he is allowed to go below. On Sunday all hands are called and mustered at the same time as on the working days, the hammocks are brought up and stowed, and the decks cleanly swept, after which the prisoners return to their wards, and breakfast is then served down. At nine all the prisoners are mustered in divisions on the main deck, for the purpose of seeing that their persons are clean and their clothing kept in proper repair. The steward also, during the week, as opportunities offer, sees that the repairing of the clothing is not neglected, and also issues clothing to those who need it. Divine service is performed by the chaplain once every Sunday. The surgeon or his assistant visits the ship daily. A book is kept in the office, in which is entered a full detail of every day's occurrences.....

The surgeon on board the hulk at Ned's time of disposal, reported on the condition and behaviour of each prisoner. Ned's report is brief, but indicates that he was in good health and behaved himself.

Leviathan Muster - 1835

Ned remained on the *Leviathan* for almost seven months. In that time he would have experienced hard labour, seen cruel punishments and lived in crowded and miserable surroundings. It would have gone some way to preparing him for a life that would involve far harder work and a lot less comfortable living conditions than on board the hulk.

MEDICAL and SURGICAL JOURNAL of His Majesty's *Convict Ship, Recovery*

between the *1st day of October 1835* and the *14th March 1836* during which

time the said *Ship* has been employed in *Passage to Sydney New South Wales*

Nature of Disease.	No. of Case.	Men's Names, Ages, Qualities, Time when and where taken ill, and how disposed of.	The History, Symptoms, Treatment, and Daily Progress of the Disease or Hurt.
Spasmodic Diarrhea	1	*Charles Seaman aged 22 taken ill on the 27th October at Sea and discharged to duty...*	*Complained in the evening of having been much purged and griped during the day...*

Across the Seas to Exile

His Majesty's Convict Ship Recovery

Ned had the good fortune to be making the long and dangerous sea voyage to New South Wales at the right time in the history of convict transportation.

Trained naval surgeons had been introduced first into the hulks and then onto every single convict vessel.

It was mandatory, after 1815, to have a Surgeon Superintendent in charge of the welfare of the ship. They had an incentive to land as many live convicts in Australia as possible, in that they received a bonus payment for doing so. They also had to issue a "please explain" if the death rate was high, and disturbing reports could result in unfavourable recommendations, which could blunt their future employment prospects.

This was the first of four voyages Alexander Neill undertook as surgeon on a convicts ship. On this voyage he kept a Medical Journal from 5 October 1835 to 16 March 1836.

A great deal of information on surgeon superintendents is available through ;
The British National Archives http://www.nationalarchives.gov.uk/surgeonsatsea/
Free Settler or Felon? website https://www.jenwilletts.com/surgeon_superintendents.htm

On the 5th October 1835, the Guard for *His Majesty's Convict Ship Recovery*, consisting of a Sergeant, a drummer and 26 rank and file of the 28th regiment, under the command of Lieut. Russell and Ensign Smith (or Swift); 8 women and three children, embarked at Deptford.

The *Recovery* was built at Batavia in 1799. She was a fast sailing, teak ship of 493 tons. Taken as a prize in the early 1800s, she had been sold to a private owner for merchant use. *Recovery* made three voyages of convict transportation, of which the 1835-36 voyage was the last.

On the 19th October, at Spithead, 160 male convicts from the *Leviathan*, including Edmund Collins and William Brown, and 120 from the *York* Hulks were transferred to *His Majesty's Convict Ship Recovery* for the voyage to NSW.

It is fortunate that the Surgeon's journal for that journey survives. It contains not only the records of all the convicts, crew or military personnel who reported sick, or died, during the voyage, but also a wealth of information about the journey itself; the weather, conditions on board, latitudes and longitudes crossed and when, and an account of various happenings on board.

It was always dangerous to be at sea, but it was less dangerous to be on a convict vessel than on a free immigrant ship. The other reason for death rates being lower is the pre-voyage checks made by the surgeons.

The surgeons had introduced disease control methods that were strictly adhered to during the voyage. They believed that disease was carried by bad smells, so the decks were scrubbed, convicts were washed with seawater, their clothes were washed. While the surgeons didn't know the scientific reasons for the spread of diseases, all of these measures were quite effective. The surgeon on the *Recovery* was Alexander Neill. He was a fine naval surgeon. In 1824 the Caledonian Mercury under the heading of Naval Promotions and Appointments - Alexander Neill, formerly a Surgeons' Mate, had been promoted to Assistant Surgeon. Four years later he was serving as assistant surgeon on the Sybille off the coast of Africa. The following report on the standard of his care appeared in a British newspaper.[15]

> *"On Thursday the Esk, Captain Purchas, arrived in Portsmouth from the coast of Africa. The Esk left Sierra Leone on 5th January in company with the Sybille and the Black Joke. In running down the Coast, they captured a Spanish slave vessel with 175 negros. The merchant seamen at Sierra Leone had suffered much from sickness arising principally from the indiscretion of the Master actively employing their crew, without the precaution of providing awnings to the boats in the heat of the day. The Surry of London had sent sixteen men to the Hospital set up at Sierra Leone, then under the charge of Mr. Alexander Neill, Assistant Surgeon of the Sybille, and on investigating the cause of their illness, Mr. Neill learnt that they had in a short space of time discharged a large cargo; that they had proceeded up the River to take in timber many exposed in the upper part of their bodies to the sun while the lower parts was immersed in water, whilst others were in the hold stowing away the timber, exposed to the damp and miasma. Mr. Neill was successful in his mode of treatment, and had been generally so, having on a former occasion restored to health, seven out of eight of another vessel's crew.. The North Star and the Primrose were cruising in the Bight of Benin." - Hampshire Telegraph, 3rd May 1828*

Alexander Neill was promoted to the position of surgeon on 27 October 1830. He was employed as surgeon superintendent on the convict ships Heber, 1837, Parkfield, 1839, and Eden 1842 as well as this voyage on Recovery in 1836.

The following are his general remarks, recorded in the Surgeons Journal for the *Recovery*, on the leaving of England.

> *"On 5th October 1835, the Guard embarked at Deptford, consisting of 1 staff, 1 subaltern, 2 sergeants, 1 drummer, 26 rank and file of the 28th Regiment, accompanied by 8 women and 4 children. On the 19th at Spithead we received on board 160 male convicts from the Leviathan and 120 from the York Hulk and in the 30th got under weigh, previous to which, two convicts were discharged to the hulks in consequence of their being a great nuisance on board from incontinence of urine and foul excreting from filth. Ten others were changed by order of the Secretary of State."*

The Recovery weighed anchor on 30 October 1835 with 280 male prisoners. The surgeon reported that the prisoners suffered from sea sickness in the early part of November which was exacerbated by the cocoa they were fed and of which they had the greatest possible dislike and disgust. He recommended that cocoa was not a fit ration to give to convicts and that oatmeal, which the convicts looked on as a luxury, would be a better choice.

The weather remained fine throughout November and December, and there was little illness on board although one of the soldiers who had been despondent lost all recollection at this time. He remained in a cataleptic state and died on 4th February. Alexander Neill recorded in his journal that nine prisoners were affected with symptoms of scurvy on arrival - spongy gums, macular on the extremities and, in one case, contraction of the muscles of both legs.

The Surgeon's Journal is not the only document that contains valuable information. Each convict ship's records included an indent, a list of all the prisoners on board, with full details of each one; their crime, their trial, their sentence and their physical description. It is a gold mine of information, some of which is unavailable elsewhere.

Edmund's details[16] read:

Standing No: 36-774 | Indent No:153 | Name: Edmund Collins | Age :18 | R & W (read and write) |
Protestant | Single | Children: None | Native Place: Berkshire | Trade: Baker's Boy |

Edmund is described as having five blue dots on the back of his hand. This is similar to tattoos found on many convict bodies. It has been suggested by some researchers that blue dots could also signify membership of a gang.[17] Indeed, Edmund was a member of a gang of highway robbers. However, there is no mention of five dots on the two men convicted with him. William Brown had a single blue dot on the back of his hand. It is more likely that the dots signify imprisonment, common to other convicts' tattoos. The blue line and the burn marks on his wrist may have been the result of his trade. They were most likely the caused by catching his wrist on the edge of baking tins and paddles as he removed bread from the ovens.

Edmund's behaviour is described in the surgeon's report as orderly. We can assume that he was not only well behaved, but healthy and hard working as there are no mentions of him in the surgeons' journals, or any other reports, for disciplinary or health issues on either the hulk or the convict transport ship Recovery.

The Sydney Herald reported that;

"*The Recovery camc into port on 25 February 1836 in a very creditable manner, both to her commander, Captain Johnson, and Dr Neill. The prisoners were all in a healthy condition, not one convict death having occurred during the voyage. The whole of the berths in the ship presents almost the extreme of cleanliness and the general appearance of the convicts of the same character.*"

The prisoners were held on the vessel for twenty days before being disembarked. They were landed on 16th March 1836. In this extract from *A Narrative of the sufferings of J. Loveless,* convict John Standfield, one of the Tolpuddle Martyrs, gives a description of his disembarkation from the convict ship *Surry* in 1834,

"*On the 4th of September were conveyed on shore, and marched four a-breast to Hyde Park Barracks, where we found about 300 (what they called) old hands—men, if possible, worse than those with whom we had already been associated...*"

You can read more about Stanfield's experiences here -

https://www.jenwilletts.com/john_standfield.htm

Stanfield was fortunate in being almost immediately assigned to a settler in the Hunter Valley. This was not to be Ned's fate. He was to remain assigned as a government convict, to labour.

Edmund, our Ned, would remain at Hyde Park Barracks for some time.

The Early Years

1836 - 1837

When the *Recovery* sailed into Port Jackson, it deposited the 18 year-old Ned Collins into a rapidly growing young country, with all its attendant social issues and growing pains. Ned would play his part in building Australia's future.

The colony was 48 years old when Ned arrived. It officially covered half of Australia, including Queensland, Victoria and the Northern Territory. In reality, it included the land that had been settled; the coastal and inland area within about 250 kilometres of Sydney, from Port Macquarie in the north to Queanbeyan in the south and inland as far as the Wellington Valley. New South Wales also included the fledgling settlements of Melbourne and Geelong and the convict settlements of Moreton Bay and Norfolk Island. In 1836, Sydney and NSW were very different to the town and colony that had been the landing place for the convicts of the late 18th century and the 1820s.

23 years before Ned arrived, the Blue mountains had been crossed.

The Great North Road was well underway and almost completed. Vast tracts of rich and fertile lands had opened up to the north in the Hunter and to the west towards Bathurst. The Illawarra to the south was growing. New South Wales was flourishing.

The days of a society made up of convicts and military personnel and their families were long over. In 1836, New South Wales had a non-Indigenous population of about 77,000 people, made up of convicts, ex-convicts and their families, free settlers, immigrants and military and government employees.

There were already two generations of non-indigenous Australians living in the colony. Mutterings of unrest that convicts were still being sent to Australia were becoming louder and a strong movement had started for transportation to cease.

By 1836 Bishop Polding had brought 13 Catholic primary schools into operation. Seven for boys, six for girls and all had government support. The foundation stone for a church at Parramatta had been laid.

Thanks to John Macarthur's work in the previous decade, demand for wool was driving the expansion of colonisation, including into western Victoria. The pastoral industry had become the most profitable industry in the Australian colonies, and the economy of New South Wales was centred on the production of wool for the British market. Sydney, in 1836, was a busy administrative and mercantile centre. A network of streets and wharves filled up the land around what is now Circular Quay.

Compare Sydney Cove in the 1700s to Sydney Cove when Ned arrived in 1836.

Hyde Park Barracks controlled all convicts; those arriving on the transport ships, working for the government or on private farms, those who fell back into crime, feared secondary punishment, or dreamed of freedom. It was the place where they found themselves going down the path to the freedom or a life of imprisonment. Two-thirds of the convicts in the colony were out working for private masters. The Principal Superintendent of Convicts, Frederick Augustus Hely, kept track of the whereabouts of every individual, and controlled the movement of convicts being transferred between the barracks and other penal establishments.[18]

On disembarking from the *Recovery* at Port Jackson, probably because his crime and sentence were severe and required greater punishment, Ned was assigned to "Government" in Sydney. Government convicts made up only a small group. Only hardened criminals and those who had skills needed in the city remained in Sydney. According to the Convict Muster of 31st December 1837, he was still there more than 12 months later.

Convict Muster 1837

NSW State Records

Note:

Edmund's name is recorded as *Collins, Edward* on the muster. Another example of mistakes in recording that can take time to unravel or create roadblocks.

Ned's Life in Hyde Park Barracks

By 1836, Deputy Superintendent Timothy Lane had just taken charge of the barracks. He managed the place with an iron fist. Life at the barracks under Lane was an awful existence. Many convicts 'bolted' from the barracks and worksites.

Their day started when the convicts arrived in the mess halls for breakfast. The meal consisted of half a pound (227 grams) of maize meal with 1 ounce (28 grams) of sugar for each man, mixed into a form of porridge, called hominy. Any convict who had tea leaves, and a penny, could pay the barracks' cook to boil some water to make tea. With food in their bellies, and already weary, government convicts marched out every morning after the bell called them to muster. For most, the work was dreary, back-breaking and hazardous.

Dinner was a fatty, salty stew, made with 1 pound (454 grams) of fresh beef and a quarter of an ounce (7 grams) of salt for each man, and a few vegetables. There was plenty of bread, which was fortunate, because the cooks, bakers and storemen, were known to take some of the prisoners' beef, sugar and soap for their own use. Each day, the rations were carted into the barracks, and the storekeeper stacked the sacks and crates onto the shelves in his store. He was also kept busy, day and night, protecting the stores from hordes of rats. A storekeeper once reported he had killed 352 rats in one month!

On Sundays, the convicts mustered to attend the mandatory church services. The Protestants crossed the road to St James' Church. The Catholics marched down to St Mary's Chapel. At church, convicts joined ticket-of-leave holders and married convicts living outside the barracks, who were also required to be there.

Sleeping conditions were appalling. The convicts were hopelessly overcrowded. Beneath the floorboards of the dormitories, hundreds of rats made nests, drawn to the warmth and scraps of bread stashed away by convicts. The roof leaked, dripping all night on the sleepers below, and many of the hammocks were filthy. The glass in the windows was broken, and the heat in the summer and cold in the winter filled the buildings.

Life in Hyde Park Barracks was a miserable existence and fraught with danger of illness, injury and death.

During the "icy winter" of 1836, on June 28th, the thousands of convicts in Hyde Park awoke to snow "nearly an inch deep" on June 28. *"About seven o'clock in the morning a drifting fall covered the streets,"* The Sydney Herald reported at the time. *"A razor-keen wind from the west blew pretty strongly at the time, and all together, it was the most English like winter morning ... ever experienced."*

The Sydney Monitor, said: *"We believe snow was never seen in Sydney before the previous night."* The meteorological table in The Sydney Herald recorded that, on the morning of the snow, the temperature dropped to three degrees Celsius (or 38 degrees Fahrenheit).

METEOROLOGICAL TABLE.

The Weather, and variation of the Thermometer since last day's publication, in Sydney, at 6 in the morning, at noon, and at 6 o'clock in the evening.

	6 a. m.	12 noon.	6 p. m.
MONDAY	Cloudy 46 S W	Cloudy 50 N W	Cloudy 48 S W
TUESDAY	Snow 38 S W	Windy 50 S W	Cloudy 47 S W
WEDNESDAY	Clear 42 S W	Fine 54 S W	Clear 49 S W
Mean Temperature 47.			

We don't know the specific work Ned carried out during his time in Sydney. With a 14 year sentence he was considered a hardened criminal and would not have been considered for assignment to a free settler. He was there to be punished for a very serious crime and hard labour would have been his lot.

However, he must have been of good behaviour and proved trustworthy, because the next time we see Ned in the records, it is 1843 and he is in Wollongong, south of Sydney.

Wollengong.

From the Stockade. April 26. 1840.

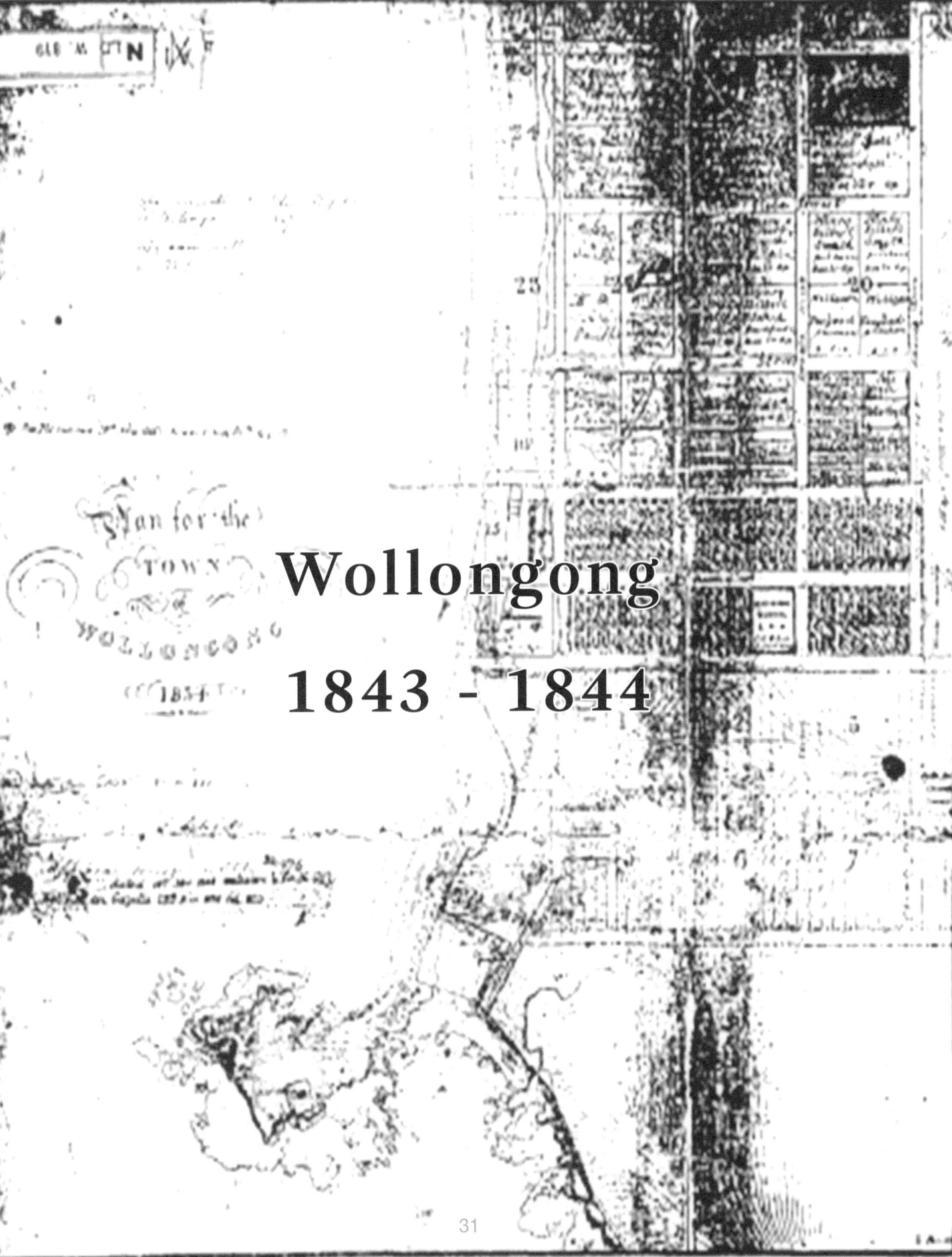

Wollongong

1843 - 1844

In 1843, Wollongong was expanding. The foundation for the town of Wollongong, and the plan for its development, had been laid down in 1834. Although pioneer settlers had established homes and properties in the area from Thirroul to Dapto, roads were rough tracks and there was little infrastructure. The escarpment, dividing the Southern Highlands and Campbelltown to the west from the coastal strip, made travel to and from these settlements, and Sydney to the north, extremely difficult. With a new town to be built, infrastructure had to be provided for the public services of transport, administration, law enforcement and protection.[19]

In order to move settlers to and from Sydney, or to send produce from the farms to market there, it was necessary to take them by ship from 'Boat Harbour', known today as Belmore Basin. The ships would stand out to sea. Goods and people were rowed out in small flat bottom boats for loading. Rough weather and high seas made this a hazardous operation and handicapped the economic development of the town.

The new plan included the construction of a harbour with a breakwater. It is entirely possible that Ned was one of this gang of convicts, or one of the later gangs brought down from Sydney to work on road construction to the north and south of the town.

It was probably a relief for the convicts from Sydney to get out of Hyde Park. However, the living conditions in Wollongong were far from salubrious and not much of an improvement on the barracks.

Convict work gangs were housed in 'stockades' close to their place of work. The stockades had high fences around them. Convict living quarters were wooden boxes, somewhat similar to caravans. They were mobile, approximately 3.5 metres wide x 5 metres long x 2 metres high. They could house 24-28 men in 4 rows of 6 with one shared urinal. They were very cramped, with no mattresses on the bunks, only blankets. Convicts were locked in these when not out working.

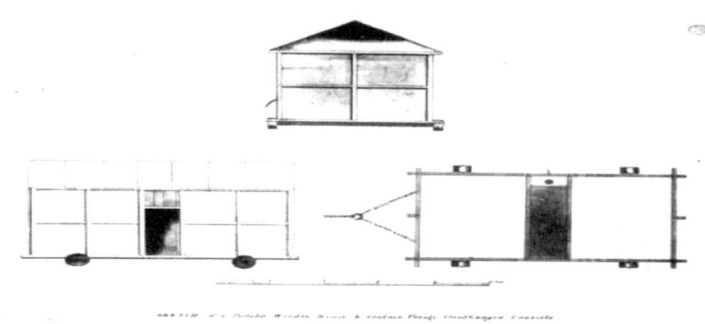

In 1837, Governor Bourke instructed the Colonial Engineer, Captain George Barney of the Royal Engineers, to design and oversee the construction of a harbour at Wollongong. Barney's design was for a basin 100 ft long, 35 feet wide and 8 feet deep at low tide, with a stone pier that incorporated a slipway for the Pilot Boat, on the northern side at the sheltered end of Boat Harbour. The excavation was to be carried out by drilling and blasting behind a coffer dam.

It was reported in 1841, after construction commenced in 1837, that the size of the basin was to be increased to 300 feet long and 150 feet wide.

Later in the year about 300 convicts, accompanied by a guard of soldiers under Captain Plunkett, were sent down to begin construction.

There were three stockades in the Illawarra. One on Flagstaff Hill above the harbour for the harbour workers, one at the bottom of Mt Keira housing the work gangs for Mt Keira Road and one at Dapto for the convicts working on the road to Kiama, Gerringong and the south.

In May 1839, Lady Jane Franklin visited the convict stockade at Wollongong. In her diary she reported[20] ;

"The barracks and huts of the prisoners are here. We looked into the huts, etc. There are about 115 convicts here and about 30 troops of the 80th Regiment. Captain Rait is the Commandant. The men are lodged in wooden 'boxes' forming the side of a square on the tongue of land which was the only part Sir Richard Bourke would accept from Mr Smith. There are 5 or 6 of these 'boxes', with no windows, and holding 24 each. No light or air enters them but from iron bars at the top of the door. Men were lying on the bare floors and on bare wooden platforms alone. We were told they were locked in only at night, but found them locked in now. We saw no mattresses. 'Have they none?' we asked the soldiers.
'Only the sick', was their reply.

There is a further description of a typical stockade in Grace Karsens' "The Convict Road Station Site at Wisemans Ferry: an Historical and Archaeological Investigation"

In August 1843 Ned made an application to marry Catherine Brogan, an Irish immigrant girl from County Cavan. The application was granted and they were married. One of the witnesses at their wedding was Frederick Wyatt, a baker of Wollongong who was a Ticket-of-Leave man. They were probably friends.

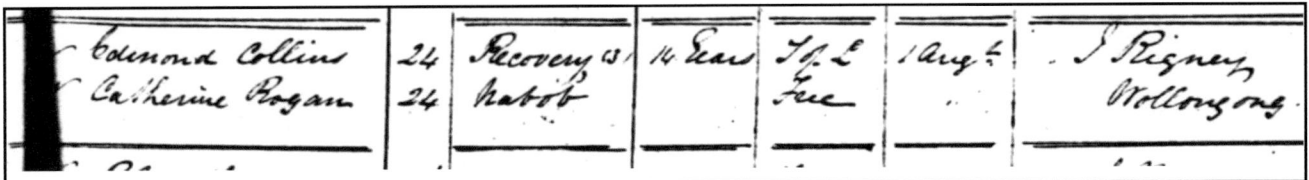

Note: This was a very difficult record to find as Catherine's name was mis-spelled as "Rogan", rather than "Brogan"
When the Convict Permissions to Marry database was first released, my initial search was "Edmund Collins AND Catherine Brogan". This brought up 0 records. At that time, we did not know Edmund was a convict and assumed it was another dead end in a 20 year search for his arrival. It was not until we later searched for his name alone that the record was found. This led me to all of the other convict records and was the breakthrough.
Lesson:-Brick walls eventually yield as new records are released. Keep on trying!!

Catherine had arrived in the colony aboard the Nabob in 1842 as an Irish Bounty Immigrant, under the protection of the Crawford family, a couple and their three children, who came from the same town.

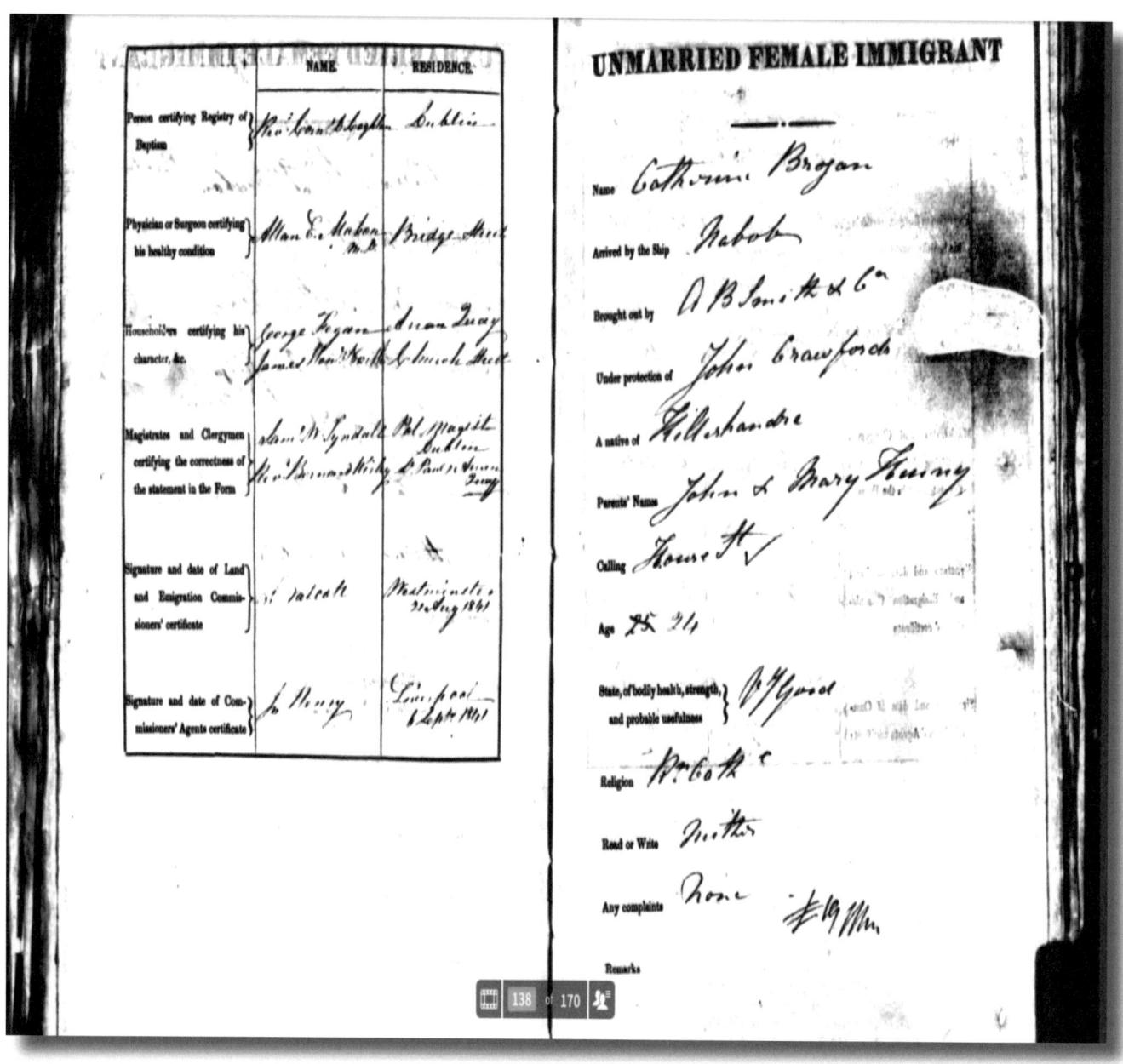

She was 24 years old. Her parents were John Brogan and Mary Henny.

Catherine had the dubious honour of being mentioned in despatches by the surgeon superintendent on the *Nabob*. There is a record in the surgeon's report of Catherine keeping watch at the door, while her friend was "occupied" with the 2nd Mate in the hospital. She was used as an example of the poor quality of female Bounty Immigrants chosen by the Immigration Board to travel to New South Wales.[21]

Their first child, Edmond was born in that same year. Whether prior to, or within four months of the wedding, obviously Catherine was pregnant prior to their marriage. Catherine seems to have had a certain amount of spirit and courage. Over the next few years she would need it.

Ned remained a Government convict until 13th November, 1844 when he received his Ticket of Leave (TOL).This meant that Ned was now living in Campbelltown. It is quite possible that he was assigned to Catherine, as she was a free settler. In any event, Edmund Collins, baker, and his wife Catherine were in Campbelltown around the time that Ned received his TOL. [22]

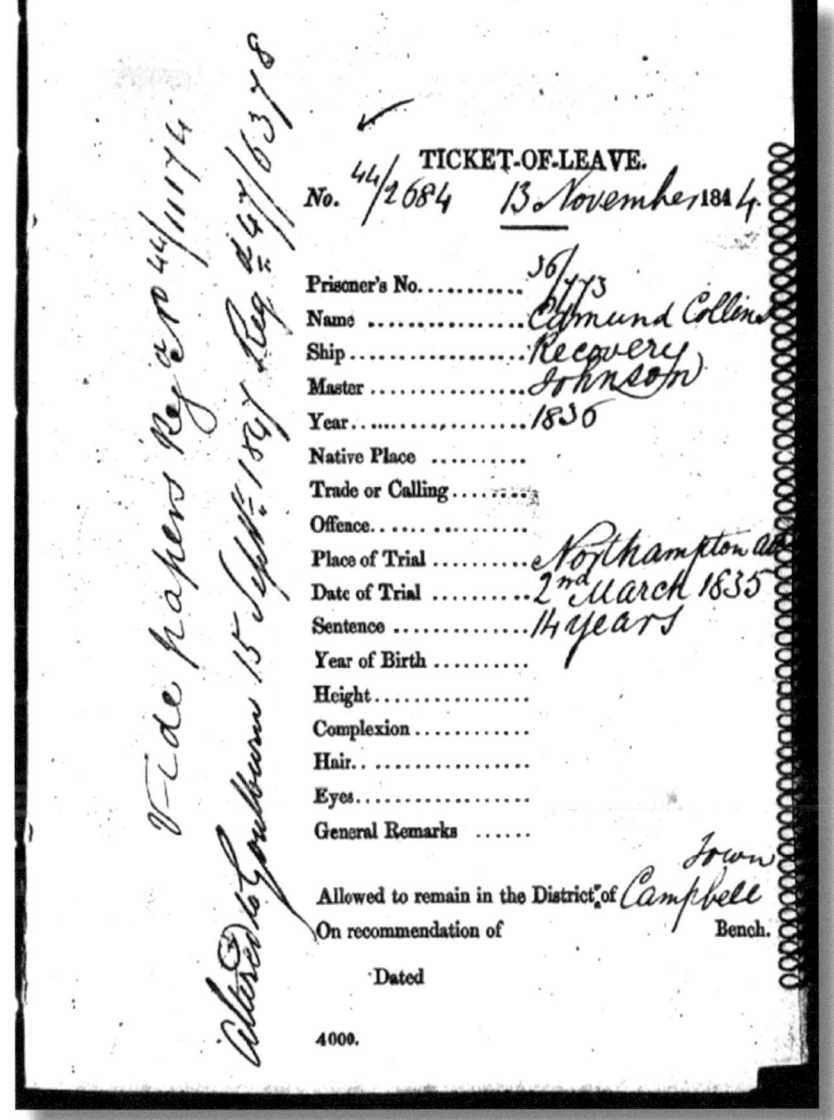

Ticket of Leave No. 44/2684
13th November 1844
Prisoner's No.... 36/773
Name...Edmund Collins
Ship... Recovery
Master... Johnson
Year...1835

Place of Trial... Northampton
Date of Trial... 2nd March 1835
Sentence... 14 years

Allowed to remain in the District of Campbelltown.

V[?]-ide Papers Reg'd 44/11174
There is an annotation made in 1847
Altered to Goulburn 15th Sept. 1847 Regd 47/6378

In 1845, Daniel Collins their second son was born. He lived only a year. He was buried at St Peter's Church of England on 9th October 1846.

Their third child, a daughter, Ann, was born in 1846. All three of these children were born in Campbelltown.

There is an annotation, made in 1847, on Ned's Ticket of Leave. It reads "Altered to Goulburn 15th September 1847". Ticket of Leave convicts had to request permission to move to another place.

On the 17th of December 1847, there is a landmark change in Ned's life. He receives his Conditional Pardon.[23] His sentence is over. Ned is now a free man, free to move where he likes and do what he wishes. The only restriction on him is that he can never return to England or the British Isles.

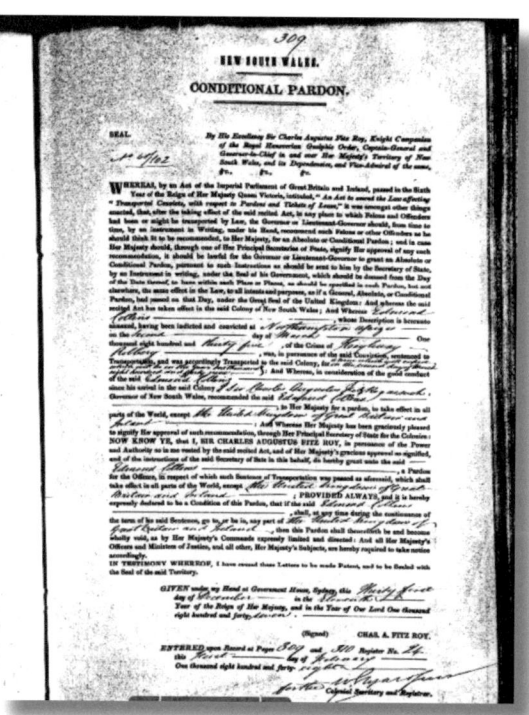

Ned's Conditional Pardon
NSW State Archives

Another son, William, was born in 1848 and registered in Campbelltown. Whether Ned went to Goulburn alone and left Catherine to follow after William's birth, we do not know. We believe it most likely that the family moved to Goulburn after William was born.

In 1848, a Goulburn Confectionery and Bakery business was owned by Mr. H. Wilson. In Mr Wilson's advertisement in the Goulburn Herald is a line advertising work for a Pastry Cook and Confectioner. [24]

It could be that Ned went to work for Mr Wilson and learnt advanced confectionery skills from him, but the gap between 1848 and the announcement of the opening of Ned's shop remains a mystery. I can find no records relating to the family in that period.

By May 1849, Ned was a Confectioner and Baker in Goulburn.

In the mid-1800s confectionery was the most highly regarded of all the trades involved in the preparation of food. Their skills were considered to be of a more elevated order than those of a mere cook or baker and if they were successful in the craft they could command not only impressive financial rewards, but a respectable social standing usually denied to other food professionals. Confectioners made more than just bread. Their shops were an Aladdin's cave of sweet treats.

EDMUND COLLINS,

PASTRY-COOK,

CONFECTIONER,

Fancy Bread and Biscuit Baker,

SLOANE STREET,

NEAR MR. MANDELSON'S HOTEL, GOULBURN.

BEGS leave to inform the inhabitants of the surrounding districts, that he has removed to the above commodious premises, where he is prepared to supply

Every Article in the Confectionary line

EQUAL TO THE BEST HOUSES IN

SYDNEY AND LONDON.

Lozenges one shilling per pound
Common Sweetmeats nine pence per ditto
Cordials of every description at six shillings per gal.
First quality Biscuit eighteen shillings per cwt.
☞ Wedding and Christening Cakes at the shortest Notice.

Goulburn Herald and County of Argyle Advertiser (NSW : 1848 - 1859),

Saturday 15th May 1849

In 1849, Ned opened his own establishment in a prestigious part of Goulburn and traded as a Confectioner. Ned's Goulburn shop was in Sloane St, a popular spot for business. It was close to Mandelson's Hotel which was a high class establishment. The shop was owned by Mendelson's and rented by Edmund. In his Goulburn shop, Ned would have made;

- Sweetmeats - , sherbet lemons, aniseed twists, marshmallows, candy floss and fruit gums, candied fruits, comfits.

- Lozenges - cough drops, lemon drops, fruit pastilles, peppermints

- Boiled sweets - fruit drops, peppermint rock, humbugs, toffee, pear drops,rhubarb and custard drops.

- Biscuits, cakes, scones

- White and brown bread, buns and rolls.

- Cordials - a sugary flavoured syrup for making drinks.

However, Goulburn was not the ideal place to start a new business. In 1849 there were a number of Confectioners trading in the town, and all were competing strongly for customers. A search of classifieds revealed that three of these, Mr Henry Grieg, Mr. W. Kingsell and Mr Lawrence had been established in Goulburn for some time and were advertising aggressively.

Historical Research - Goulburn in 1849 was recovering from difficult economic times. As people earned less, shops faced difficulties selling goods. A slump in land sales, falling prices and lower incomes resulted in an upsurge of insolvencies that substantially weakened the banks. Stock and land were hard to sell due to the drought. Goulburn was a town that prospered because of the wool trade. The Squattocracy was centred around the Goulburn Plains. Speculators who bought land expecting its value to rise found that they were no longer able to sell or repay their mortgages to the bank.

The early 1840s saw the first bank failures in Australia. By 1845, NSW was returning to better times, Goulburn started to come recover. In 1849 the Goulburn newspaper had just been established.

In this economic climate, starting a new business in a market with established and successful competitors and a population struggling with hard times was a task doomed to failure.

As a newcomer to town, and someone who was not a known and trusted trader, it must have been difficult for Ned to build up a business that would support him and his family.

The following article appeared in the Goulburn Herald a month after Ned announced the opening of his Confectionery.

SHOOTING THE MOON—On Thursday night, a tenant of Mr. Mandelson's named Collins, who was carrying on business as Baker and Confectioner, in Sloane-street, took a sudden departure from his premises with his wife and child, goods and all. The most important part of the " flit" is, that in the hurry of moving, Collins forgot to settle a few accounts due by him to some of the trades-people in the town. Singular to relate, the last tenant in the same house left Goulburn in a similar manner.

Goulburn Herald and County of Argyle Advertiser (NSW : 1848 - 1859), Saturday 16 June 1849

Ned and Catherine had 'done a moonlight flit'. They had packed up the family and all their possessions and left town overnight, leaving unpaid bills and their reputations behind.

A clue as to how this sad state of affairs had come about is in the last sentence of the article. The tenant before Ned had financial problems too. Success in business was difficult at this time. It had come about because the colony was only just recovering from a severe economic depression. The colony's first pastoral boom had ended in a depression which was at its worst in the mid-1840s. Severe drought in 1838–1840 had brought the need to import wheat. Payment for imports drained money from the colony. Less money, less customers, less money equalled business failure.

We know that on leaving Goulburn the Collins family moved back to Campbelltown, as the next time they appear in the NSW records is in the St Peter's Baptismal Register recording the christening of his son George, born in 1850 and a year later, baby George's death and burial. In 1851, William, the child born in 1848, was baptised, also at St Peter's Campbelltown. The Collins family had entered the 1850s.

In order to understand what happened to them next, we need to take a broad look at what Cambelltown was like, and what was happening across the colony.

The Collins Family and Campbelltown in 1849

When they returned to Campbelltown, Edmund and Catherine had three children; Edmund, also known as Ned, who was six years old, Ann aged 3 and William just a year old. Surely now, Ned would settle down and find work as a baker in the town. Catherine had given birth to four children in the six years they had been married, and lost one baby at a year old.

It was less than a year before Catherine was pregnant again. She gave birth to George in 1850. She must have longed for some stability.

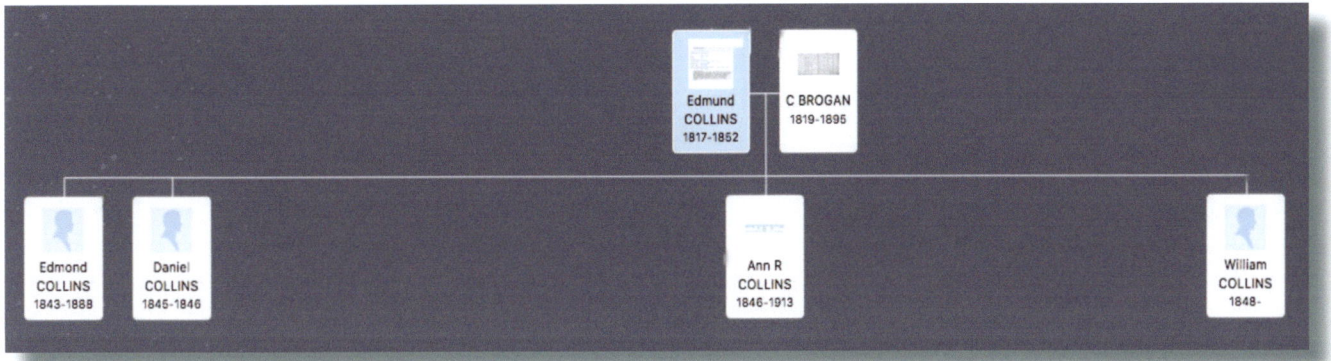

Ned was working as a baker in the town. In 1848 there were 540 people living in Campbelltown in 104 houses. That's not a huge market for a baker, but enough to earn a living unless householders baked their own.

In 1850 George French Angus, travelling through NSW, described Campbelltown as follows;

> *"From Liverpool the country improves towards Campbelltown, and as the soil becomes richer everything around has a more pleasing aspect, the surface of the land is here undulating and hills rise beyond Campbelltown...*
> *The town itself consists principally of one long street, reminding one of similar market towns in England, in which the High Street is diversified here and there with the leading inns...it is just so...in New South Wales."*

The road from Campbelltown led south to Appin and from there on to the Southern Highlands and Goulburn. The road broought travellers to town on their way to Goulburn.

A pleasant place to live, it had two churches, a circuit court, a number of Taverns and inns and an active market place. There was a small but lively community. We know from newspaper reports that Ned was an active member of the cricket team in 1850/51, a good bowler.

However, things happened in 1851 that set the family on the move again. All of New South Wales and half the world was on the move, exciting times were coming. Ned and Catherine Collins and their children were about to play their part in one of the most vibrant and exciting periods in Australia's history.

Australia in the 1850s

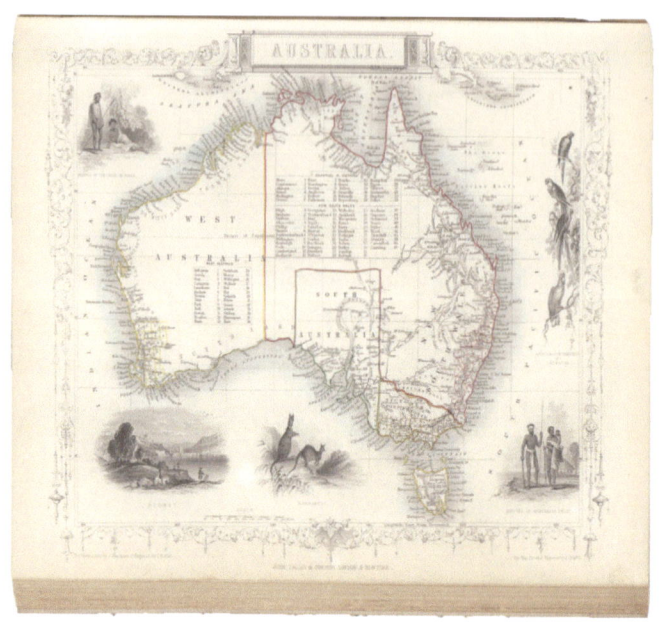

In 1851 gold was discovered in Australia, first at Bathurst in New South Wales and then in the newly formed colony of Victoria. It transformed Australia economically, politically and demographically. The gold rushes closely followed a significant global economic depression. As a result, almost two percent of the population of Britain and Ireland migrated to NSW and Victoria during the 1850s, together with large numbers of Europeans, North Americans and Chinese.

The gold rushes of the 1850s brought a massive influx of settlers. Initially, the majority of them went to Ballarat and Bendigo, in the Port Phillip District. In 1851 this area was separated to become the colony of Victoria. But the New South Wales gold fields also attracted a flood of prospectors, and by 1857 the colony had more than 300,000 people. Inland towns like Bathurst, Goulburn, Orange and Young flourished. Gold brought great wealth, but also new social tensions. Multi-ethnic migrants came to New South Wales in large numbers for the first time. Young became the site of an infamous anti-Chinese miner riot in 1861, and the official Riot Act was read to the miners on 14 July – the only official reading in the history of New South Wales. Despite some tension, the influx of migrants also brought fresh ideas from Europe and North America – Norwegians introduced skiing in Australia to the Snowy Mountains gold rush town of Kiandra around 1861. A famous Australian son was born to a Norwegian miner in 1867, when the bush balladeer Henry Lawson was born at the Grenfell gold fields. In 1858 a new gold rush began in the far north, which led to the separation of Queensland as a new colony in 1859.

Gold produced sudden wealth for a few. It also brought employment and prosperity for many more. Within a few years, new settlers outnumbered the convicts and ex-convicts, and they began to demand trial by jury, representative government, a free press and the other symbols of liberty and democracy.

Before 1850, large areas of the inland were still unknown to Europeans. Explorers made some of the last great expeditions into the interior of Australia in this decade - some with the official sponsorship of the colonial authorities and others commissioned by private investors. Trailblazers like Edmund Kennedy and Ludwig Leichhardt met tragic ends attempting to fill in the gaps during the 1840s, but explorers remained ambitious to discover new lands for agriculture or to answer scientific enquiries. Surveyors acted as explorers and the colonies sent out expeditions to determine the best routes for lines of communication. The size of expeditions varied from small parties of just two or three to large, well-equipped teams led by gentlemen explorers assisted by smiths, carpenters, labourers and Indigenous guides, with horses, camels or bullocks as their means of transport.

In 1855 New South Wales, Victoria, South Australia and Tasmania (as Van Diemen's Land was renamed) were granted full responsible government, with parliaments in which the lower houses were wholly elected. The upper houses (Legislative Councils) remained dominated by government appointees and representatives of the squatters.

Australia was taking shape and growing up as a nation. Ned and Catherine were bringing up their family and participating in all of its excitement, enthusiasm and, sometimes, tragedy.

Time Line of events from 1850 - 1862

1850   Western Australia becomes a penal colony.
University of Sydney founded.
Australian Colonies Government Act passed.
Railway from Sydney to Goulburn built.

1851   Separation of Victoria from New South Wales.
Hargreaves digs for gold on Summerhill Creek.
Gold found at Ballarat.
The diggings commence.

1852   University of Melbourne founded.

1853   Tasmania named.
Town of Gladstone founded.
French annexation of New Caledonia.

1854   The Eureka Stockade.
Hobson's Bay railway built.

1855   Transportation to Norfolk Island ceased.

1855   New constitutions come into effect in New South Wales, Victoria,
South Australia, and Tasmania.
Ballot Act passed in Victoria.
First anti-Chinese legislation passed.

1858   Torrens Real Property Act passed.

1859   Colony of Queensland proclaimed.
Kingsley's "Geoffrey Hamlyn" published.

1860   McDouall Stuart reaches the centre of the continent.

1861   Burke and Wills expedition. Cowper's quarrel with the New South Wales Legislative Council.

1862   McDouall Stuart crosses the continent to Port Darwin.

Trove
https://trove.nla.gov.au

One of the richest sources of information on life in Australia at any given time is the Australian National Library . Through Trove, the ANL online service, access is available to;

- digitised newspapers,
- diaries,
- letters,
- photographs,
- journals,
- Government Gazettes,
- music, sound and video and
- many other forms of material that help us to understand how our ancestors lived.

Gold Fields, Sofala

1851-1862

NSW Gold Rush

The NSW Gold Rush began in 1851 with Edward Hargraves' discovery of payable gold at Summer Hill Creek, near Bathurst.

Hargraves left his colleagues digging at the field they had called Ophir at a point of the Summerhill Creek near its junction with the Macquarie, to travel some fifty miles into Bathurst to break the news of their discoveries.

The first gold in Sofala was found by two men, Lester and Raffael at Golden Point, 3/4 mile east of the village, three weeks after the Ophir strike in 1851.

In that year New South Wales' population was about 200,000 people, a third of them within a day's ride of Sydney, the rest scattered along the coast and through the rural districts, from Port Phillip in the south to Moreton Bay in the north.

William Bayley's book, 'History of Campbelltown: New South Wales', [25] reports the leaving of Campbelltown in 1851 of Ned Collins, a baker, with a group of men walking to the gold fields at Summer Hill.

"Some of those residents were lost with the opening of the gold diggings in 1851. Wm Bursill years afterwards told the story of the departure of the party from Campbelltown on May 25, 1851 to travel to the new gold field at "Summer Hill." The party included Ned Collins, Jack Haray, William Williams, Bursill snr, Wm Bursill and a lad of 15 years to mind camp and cook. They travelled across country to Penrith, crossed the Nepean River there by punt and camped on the road over the Blue Mountains in the rush to the diggings. Campbelltown during the succeeding twenty years was both to lose and to win by the goldrushes; losing men and benefiting by the traffic passing through to the gold fields."

William A. Bayley, History of Campbelltown: NSW

Catherine either accompanied him on this arduous journey or followed, as in 1852 baby George's death was registered in Bathurst, NSW. They settled at Golden Point, on Summerhill Creek, close to Sofala. Conditions at Golden Point in 1852 were hard, with tents the predominant form of dwelling. The weather was harsh. Dysentery, pneumonia and influenza were rife. Little wonder that a toddler succumbed.

Goldwashing at Summerhill Creek, 1851 by George French Angas.

The following are newspaper reports from the diggings in NSW in February 1852. They give a tragic picture of the area in which Ned and Catherine lived.

" *THE TURON.*

If an earthquake had devastated the region of the Turon, its effects could scarcely have been more disastrous than those occasioned by the floods of the past week.

On Sunday, the 25th instant, the rain set in, and by the following morning the long-cherished hopes of hundreds of anxious and expectant men were doomed to a cruel blight. Many, after expending all they were worth on their bed claims, and had been practising most rigorously the virtue of self-denial in the endurance of most severe toils, arose to witness their labours of weeks rendered utterly fruitless, and covered by an angry torrent. For five days it rained almost unceasingly, completely flooding both the Turon and its tributaries, and drenching the face of the country. But the loss of their labour was not all, everything in the shape of comfort completely disappeared. Wet under foot, wet over head, ankle deep in water or liquid mud, the miners had to eat, sleep, work or play,water-soaked and miserable. The frail tents of hundreds afforded but an insufficient protection to the inclemency of the weather, and predisposed as many of them are to disease, from hard labour at the bottom of deep holes, and constantly wet; others from habitual dissipation, and not a few from general negligence to diet, personal cleanliness, and so forth, dysentery has been making fearful havoc amongst them, sending numbers of men in the very bloom of their existence to a premature grave. On Thursday last no fewer than a dozen funerals had taken place, and orders for coffins were pouring in to the joiners of Sofala almost hourly. Bed-claims being no longer workable, many of their owners are become disgusted, and are willing to sell out almost for anything. Several first rate claims have latterly changed hands on exceedingly moderate terms. M'Cormac and Davidson's party, at Ration Hill, sold their claim, tent, and implements, to a company for £100. Their gold, the produce of ten days' labor, previous to the flood, amounted to £500, and was purchased at Mr. Austin's store, Oakey Creek. Captain Bloomfield, of Sofala, bought a bedclaim, tent, implements, three months' rations, Sec., for £10, from a party who had been making 4 to 5 ozs. of gold per day, with a good prospect both of permanency and improvement. Many other claims have been disposed of on equally low terms, and notices of sale posted on the trees and rocks with which the river banks are skirted, meet the eye on every side.

As usual on such occasions, the floods have been attended with loss of life. Four dead bodies have been picked up at various parts of the river. One was found, having on only a hunting shirt, at Sheep Station Point, and interred there; another below Harbottle's store, and two others lower down the river. Several narrow escapes are also spoken of. One individual was washed a distance of three hundred yards below Sheep Station Point, and was only saved at last by the exertions of his friends, who dragged him out of the torrent in a state of exhaustion, all but dead.

A very dangerous communication has been carried on by means of ropes fastened to trees on the opposite banks of the river, by which the diggers have passed across to the township, for food and other necessaries, and in some instances, men have been known to fasten a rope round their waists, having previously thrown the other end across, and been dragged through the raging torrent to the opposite side.

In the absence of other means of employment, many of the diggers have betaken themselves to the hills and dry gullies, where they are generally earning a livelihood, and in a few cases doing more.

OPHIR.

The floods have completely put a stop to mining operations at Ophir. Since the commencement of last week's rains the water has been higher than since the first discovery of gold on Summerhill Creek. For the present, there-fore, miners are laying to, in the hope, frequently deferred, that " there's a good time coming." Mr. White has been compelled to suspend the workings at Messrs. Samuel and M'Intosh's waterhole, and, as I understand, discharged 12 men, because of the uncertainty how soon and the certainty that a considerable period most elapse ere business can be resumed. Only sufficient hands are retained to complete the requisite machinery. The water, however, is lowering very fast, and without further interruptions I doubt not but something astonishing will be done before the approach of winter's rains. Your readers may perhaps not be aware that another waterhole at the junction has been taken by a Sydney company, on whose behalf Sir Osborne Gibbes arrived here a few days ago to make the necessary preparations. He was taken rather aback upon his arrival to perceive the creek bank high. "

Bathurst Free Press February 4 1852   Australian National Library - Trove

Sofala 1851

A correspondent for the Sydney newspapers gave a description of Sofala in November 1852.

"Studding the winding bank of the Turon, a straggling village, composed of every variety of structure, from the simple white or brown canvas tent, to the substantial cedar house, which is beginning to supersede the temporary huts of slab and bark which were the chief boast of the Turon a year ago. In the midst of the town, on a slight elevation, rises the Wesleyan Chapel, a neat building of weatherboard, and the hospital of weatherboard and bark.

On a hill on the right, a canvas building, surmounted by a plain wooden cross, represents the Church of England, and close to it is a bark house, the residence of the Rev. Mr. Palmer. All along the river and creeks to the left and to the right, as far as the eye can see, huts and tents, stores and public houses, are dotted about at random, conveying a pleasing impression of the activity and bustle which has prevailed on the spot, and which, though much deadened by the influence of the very wet season, and continual floods, promises now to be greater than ever if the fine weather continues.... At various points on the river operations have already commenced, but in most cases the water is still too high to enable the digger to do any good in his claim; and most of the holders are merely making a living out of the "tailings" and waiting with exemplary patience for the drying up of the river. I witnessed the operation of rocking the cradle and extracting the gold in several instances. One digger, at Maitland Point, obtained only a few shillings' worth of the precious metal, out of thirty or forty spadesful of stuff; but he is the holder of a claim for which he gave £100 last year, and which he would not now sell for £500.

Another party of three who have just come down from Tambaroura, have scarcely made a living for the last month or two; but they told me they had claims at and about Golden Point and Oakey Creek, which they expected would yield five or six thousand pounds during the summer months. The general impression among the diggers themselves is that the bed of the river is immensely rich, and that hitherto nothing worthy the name of gold digging has been accomplished."

It would have been easy to give up and go back to Campbelltown. However, Ned and his family remained in Sofala and its surrounding district for many years, and through several generations.

According to **burial** records, Ned was buried in 1852, at the age of 45, on 17th September, after a period in Sofala Hospital.

However, this date coincides with the burial of baby George and I wonder if there has not been a transcription error, as Ned's **death** certificate is dated 1862. It remains a mystery, and, until we have further confirmation from the NSW Registrar, we have accepted the death certificate as the primary source most likely to be correct.

The family remained ordinary people. None have gained fame or fortune, that we know of. Their daughter, Ann Rebecca Collins married miner William Charters. Bill and Annie were well known in Gulgong and Sofala. Their son, Ned, was a popular man in the district and George became a bullocky. Ned's granddaughter, Ada, married John Robinson Hopwood Sutton and is the current generation's 3xGreat Grandmother.

Ned's youngest descendant is a seventh generation Australian, his 4xgreat grandchild. In 17 years her family will have seen the passage of two centuries of Australian history. She has a heritage of which she can be proud.

Registrar's can make mistakes!

Ned's burial certificate issued by NSW Births Deaths and Marriages, gives Ned's date of death as 1852, but his death certificate shows his death as 1862. I have reported the anomaly to the NSW Registrar's Office who have informed me that they will investigate.

It is not possible that the 1862 record could be the Collins' eldest son, Edmond, as a newspaper report has him present at a dance in 1865.

When meeting up with brick walls. Question everything and look carefully at the official documents. Human error can lead you on a false trail.

Descended from Australian Royalty

And so the Baker's Boy of Berkshire became the Gold Miner of Sofala. From newspaper reports in the 1850s and 1860s, we know he and his family were well thought of there, and in Molong, where his son and daughter lived and brought up families of their own.

The life and experiences of Great-great-great-great Grandpa Ned are fascinating. Research is continuing. The more we dig through the records, the more interesting his story becomes. He may have arrived in Sydney in chains, but he remained to become a part of Australian History. He saw the birth and growing pains of our country. He was there to witness the growth of pastoral industries on the Southern Highlands and take part in the NSW Gold Rush from its very beginning. He and his family remained in the Bathurst/Mudgee region, where they and other Convicts and Settlers built a strong Australian identity of farmers and graziers, bullock drivers and women of the west.

Edmund Collins' transportation to NSW gave him the opportunity to make a new life for himself and leave his criminal past behind. While struggle and hard work always seem to have been his lot in life, (and he didn't quite cease his roguish behaviour) Ned's story was very much that of any British settler since The First Fleet. He arrived, settled in, established a new way of life and living, married, worked at his trade and struggled to raise a family in tough conditions.

If our parents or grandparents knew of their convict roots, it was never mentioned. Like many family skeletons, it was kept discreetly in the cupboard. Convicts were not always regarded as altogether 'couth' by previous generations. The current generations, however, are delighted to be descended from Australian Royalty.

Good on you, Ned! We're proud to call you Grandpa, to tell your story to anyone who cares to listen.

You too can be proud. Some of your ancestors turned out to be pretty good cooks, confectioners and bakers.

"Remember me in the family tree
My name, my days, my strife;
Then I'll ride on the wings of time
And live an endless life."

Author Unknown

In loving memory of
Robert John and Warwick Walter Sutton
Great, great grandsons of Edmund (Ned) Collins

```
┌──────────────┐      ┌──────────────┐
│   Edmund     │══════│  Catherine   │
│   COLLINS    │      │   BROGAN     │
│  1817 - 1852 │      │  1819 - 1895 │
└──────────────┘      └──────────────┘

┌──────────────┐      ┌──────────────┐
│ Ann Rebecca  │══════│William George│
│   COLLINS    │      │   CHARTERS   │
│  1846 - 1913 │      │  1837 - 1903 │
└──────────────┘      └──────────────┘

┌──────────────┐      ┌──────────────┐
│     Ada      │══════│ John Robinson│
│  CHARTERS    │      │   Hopwood    │
│  1872 - 1956 │      │   SUTTON     │
│              │      │1871 - 5th June│
│              │      │     1945     │
└──────────────┘      └──────────────┘

┌──────────────┐      ┌──────────────┐
│   Preston    │══════│ Dulcie Irene │
│   George     │      │  (Known As   │
│  Wolfgang    │      │ Rene) LOVETT │
│   SUTTON     │      │  1904 - 1981 │
│  1903 - 1953 │      │              │
└──────────────┘      └──────────────┘

┌──────────────┐      ┌──────────────┐
│ Robert John  │      │Warwick Walter│
│   SUTTON     │      │   SUTTON     │
│  1944 - 2010 │      │  1948 - 2012 │
└──────────────┘      └──────────────┘
```

Preston Sutton rowing Robert and Warwick
(place unknown) Circa 1950.

Endnotes

1 Baptismal Certificate Parish Records of St Peter County of Cumberland 1846 Number 1563 Vol:31 Ann COLLINS.

2 Marriage Certificate Roman Catholic Church, Wollongong, 46/1843 V184346 123 Edmund COLLINS/Catherine BROGAN

3 **New South Wales and Tasmania, Australia, Convicts Applications to Marry, 1826 to 1851**. Edmund COLLINS/Catherine ROGAN

4 **British Library: British Newspaper Archive Online** Northampton Mercury 7th March 1835 http://www.britishnewspaperarchive.co.uk

5 London, England, Births and Baptisms, 1813-1906

6 Ancestry.com, Surrey, England, Baptisms, 1813-1912 (Provo, UT, USA, Ancestry.com Operations, Inc., 2013), Ancestry.com, http://www.Ancestry.com.

7 **Colin J. Richardson** (1972) The foundations of Bakery education in the late 19th century, The Vocational Aspect of Education, 24:57, 29-35, DOI: 10.1080/03057877280000061   http://dx.doi.org/10.1080/03057877280000061

8 **Colin J. Richardson** (1972) The foundations of Bakery education in the late 19th century, The Vocational Aspect of Education, 24:57, 29-35, DOI: 10.1080/03057877280000061   http://dx.doi.org/10.1080/03057877280000061

9 **British Library: British Newspaper Archive Online** http://www.britishnewspaperarchive.co.uk

10 **WWW.Parliament.UK** http://www.parliament.uk/about/livingheritage/transformingsociety/livinglearning/19thcentury/overview/poverty/   Contains Parliamentary information licensed under the Open Parliament Licence v3.0.

11 **Eden, Sir Frederick Morton** The State of the Poor London, 1797

12 **Convict Records** http://convictrecords.com.au

13 **British Library: British Newspaper Archive Online** Northampton Mercury 7th March 1835 http://www.britishnewspaperarchive.co.uk

14 **Jen Willetts, Free Settler or Felon?** http://www.jenwilletts.com/prison_hulk_report_1838.htm Accessed 4th June 2016

15 **British Library: British Newspaper Archive Online** Hampshire Telegraph, 3rd May 1828 http://www.britishnewspaperarchive.co.uk

16 **Jen Willetts, Free Settler or Felon?** http://www.jenwilletts.com/prison_hulk_report_1838.htm Accessed 4th June 2016

17 **Simon Barnard,** Convict Tattoos: Marked men and Women of Australia Text Publishing

18 *Hyde Park Barracks Museum* 12 Macquarie St, Sydney, NSW https://sydneylivingmuseums.com.au/hyde-park-barracks-museum

19 **Michael Organ and A.P. Doyle** January 1995 *Historical Records of the Illawarra Region of NSW, Australia 1770 - 1855* A Chronological Guide to Sources and Events University of Wollongong https://www.uow.edu.au/~morgan/ilchron2.htm accessed 5 June 2016

20 *Michael Organ (ed.),* The Illawarra Diary of Lady Jane Franklin, 10-17 May 1839 Illawarra Historical Publications 1988

21 **Log of the Nabob Feb. 1842** http://freepages.genealogy.rootsweb.ancestry.com/~sealark/lane-clarke.html

22 **NSW State Records**: New South Wales, Australia, Pardons and Tickets of Leave, 1824 – 1867 Edmund COLLINS

23 **NSW State Records**: New South Wales, Australia, Convict Registers of Conditional and Absolute Pardons, 1788 -1870

24 **Trove, Australian National Library** The Goulburn Herald and County of Argyle Advertiser (NSW : 1848 - 1859)

25 **Bayley, William** *History of Campbelltown, NSW* Campbelltown N.S.W., Campbelltown Municipal Council, 1965.

References and Attributions

British Records & Newspapers (online)

Colin J. Richardson (1972) The foundations of Bakery education in the late 19th century, The Vocational Aspect of Education, 24:57, 29-35, DOI: 10.1080/03057877280000061   http://dx.doi.org/10.1080/03057877280000061

John Tusler (1786) The London Adviser and Guide: Containing Every Instruction and Information Useful and Necessary to Persons Livingin London and Coming to Reside There. Section 2 Bakers Bread and Milk Original from Princeton University Digitized 3 Feb 2010

Northampton County Council Prison and Reformatory Records, Northampton, Northamptonshire, England.http://www.northamptonshire.gov.uk/en/councilservices/Community/archives/Documents/PDF%20Documents/Prison%20and%20reformatory% Accessed May 2016

WWW.Parliament.UK http://www.parliament.uk/about/livingheritage/transformingsociety/livinglearning/19thcentury/overview/poverty/   Contains Parliamentary information licensed under the Open Parliament Licence v3.0.

British Library: British Newspaper Archive Online Northampton Mercury 7th March 1835 http://www.britishnewspaperarchive.co.uk

Australian Convict Records

NSW State Records: New South Wales, Australia, Convict Indents, 1788 -1842 Ancestry.com

New South Wales, Australia Convict Ship Muster Rolls and Related Records, 1790-1849 Edmund COLLINS Ancestry.com

New South Wales and Tasmania, Australia, Convicts Applications to Marry, 1826 to 1851. Edmund COLLINS/Catherine ROGAN

NSW State Records: New South Wales, Australia, Pardons and Tickets of Leave, 1824 – 1867 Edmund COLLINS

NSW State Records: New South Wales, Australia, Convict Registers of Conditional and Absolute Pardons, 1788 -1870

NSW State Records: New South Wales, Australia, Pardons and Tickets of Leave, 1824 – 1867

New South Wales Records, Other

NSW State Records: New South Wales, Australia, Immigration Shipping List Reel 387 Nabob 2nd February 1842

State Library of New South Wales Goldwashing at Summerhill Creek, 1851 by George French Angas. Sketches in Australia: plates from G. F. Angas - six views of the gold field of Ophir ... Sydney, Woolcottt, and Clarke, 1851, and original sketches by G. Lacy from the collections of the State Library of New South Wales

Australian Newspapers & Books

The Australian National Library, Trove, Government Gazette May 1845 https://trove.nla.gov.au/newspaper/page/12505082 notice of Ned Collins' Ticket of Leave

Trove, Australian National Library The Goulburn Herald and County of Argyle Advertiser (NSW : 1848 - 1859) Saturday 5 May 1849

Bathust Free Press February 4 1852 Australian National Library - Trove Accessed 12 June 2016

Bayley, William A. History of Campbelltown: New South Wales, Campbelltown N.S.W., Campbelltown Municipal Council, 1965.

NSW State Records & NSW Registrar of Birth Death & Marriage (including church records)

Marriage Certificate Roman Catholic Church, Wollongong, 46/1843 V184346 123 Edmund COLLINS/ Catherine BROGAN

Baptism Certificate Roman Catholic Church, Wollongong, 1843 V18431170 62 Edmund COLLINS

Baptism Certificate Parish Records of St Peter County of Cumberland 1845 Number 2193 Vol:62 Daniel COLLINS

Baptism Certificate Parish Records of St Peter County of Cumberland 1846 Number 1563 Vol:31 Ann COLLINS.

Baptism Certificate Parish Records of St Peter County of Cumberland 1848 Number 1680 Vol:37A William COLLINS

Parish Records of St Peter County of Cumberland Burial Certificate 1846 Number 750 Vol: 31B Daniel COLLINS

Parish Records of St Peter County of Cumberland Baptism Certificate 1850 Number 1681 Vol: 37A George COLLINS

Death Certificate 1851 Bathurst, Kelso (County of Bathurst) V1851634 118 George COLLINS

Baptism Certificate 1852 Parish Records of Sofala, county of Roxborough 1852 Number 2363 Vol:38 George COLLINS.

Burial Certificate Parish of Sofala 1852 Number 1491 Vol:38 Edmund COLLINS

Death Certificate 1862 Bathurst, Kelso (County of Bathurst) Edmund COLLINS

Websites

Convict Records - https://convictrecords.com.au accessed May 2018

Jen Willetts, Free Settler or Felon? http://www.jenwilletts.com/convict_ship_recovery_1836.htm

Wikimedia, for a number of Copyright Free images.

Old Maps Online http://www.oldmapsonline.org

Printed by Libri Plureos GmbH in Hamburg, Germany